TEACHING
FOR
TRANSFER

*A Guide for Designing Learning With **Real-World** Application*

Michael McDowell
Foreword by Jay McTighe

Solution Tree | Press

a division of
Solution Tree

555 North Morton Street
Bloomington, IN 47404
800.733.6786 (toll free) / 812.336.7700
FAX: 812.336.7790

email: info@SolutionTree.com
SolutionTree.com

Visit **go.SolutionTree.com/instruction** to download the free reproducibles in this book.

Printed in the United States of America

Library of Congress Cataloging-in-Publication Data

Names: McDowell, Michael (Michael P.), author.
Title: Teaching for transfer : a guide for designing learning with
  real-world application / Michael McDowell.
Description: Bloomington, IN : Solution Tree Press, 2020. | Includes
  bibliographical references and index.
Identifiers: LCCN 2020002264 (print) | LCCN 2020002265 (ebook) | ISBN
  9781949539936 (paperback) | ISBN 9781949539943 (ebook)
Subjects: LCSH: Transfer of training. | School-to-work transition. |
  Education--Aims and objectives. | Effective teaching. | Career
  education.
Classification: LCC LB1059 .M34 2020 (print) | LCC LB1059 (ebook) | DDC
  370.15--dc23
LC record available at https://lccn.loc.gov/2020002264
LC ebook record available at https://lccn.loc.gov/2020002265

Solution Tree

Jeffrey C. Jones, CEO
Edmund M. Ackerman, President

Solution Tree Press

President and Publisher: Douglas M. Rife
Associate Publisher: Sarah Payne-Mills
Art Director: Rian Anderson
Managing Production Editor: Kendra Slayton
Production Editor: Rita Carlberg
Content Development Specialist: Amy Rubenstein
Copy Editor: Mark Hain
Proofreader: Jessi Finn
Cover Designer: Rian Anderson
Editorial Assistants: Sarah Ludwig and Elijah Oates

Author photography by Courtney Clark

To the educators who pushed my thinking and helped me
bring all the spare parts together for this book

ACKNOWLEDGMENTS

Solution Tree Press would like to thank the following reviewers:

Paula Auble
Instructional Coach
Verrado High School
Buckeye, Arizona

Nadya Bech-Conger
Instructional Coach
Hunt Middle School
Burlington, Vermont

Cynthia Choate
Principal
Glen Forest Elementary School
Falls Church, Virginia

Erin Fedina
Supervisor of Instruction
Howell Township Public Schools
Howell, New Jersey

Anthony Grazzini
Director of PLCs and Special Projects
Cicero School District #99
Cicero, Illinois

Errin Jennings
Director of Curriculum and Instruction
Luling Independent School District
Luling, Texas

Darin Johnston
Sixth-Grade Teacher
North Fayette Valley Middle School
Elgin, Iowa

Kelly Melendez Loaiza
Science Teacher
Mansfield High School
Mansfield, Massachusetts

John Schiefer
Curriculum Support Provider
Madison Elementary School
Sanger, California

Megann Tresemer
Curriculum Professional
   Development Leader
Cedar Falls Schools
Cedar Falls, Iowa

Jake Wiese
Director of Curriculum, Instruction,
   and Assessment
Shenandoah School Corporation
Middletown, Indiana

Visit **go.SolutionTree.com/instruction** to download the free reproducibles in this book.

TABLE OF CONTENTS

ABOUT THE AUTHOR

Michael McDowell, EdD, serves as the superintendent of the Ross School District in Ross, California. During his tenure, the Ross School District has progressed to the top of California districts regarding student connectedness and well-being, as well as the top tier of districts in academic achievement and growth. The Ross School District has also emerged as a hub for innovation, creating more than sixty-five different electives—from virtual game design to broadcast journalism—sponsoring the first TEDxYouth event in the Bay Area, and establishing a service-learning and community-engagement program for all students to serve the local and global community.

Prior to serving as a superintendent, McDowell served as an associate superintendent of instructional and personnel services and as a high school principal of a Title I and California Distinguished School. Before entering administration, he was a leadership and instructional coach, consulting with schools, districts, higher educational institutions, and state departments on educational leadership, teaching leadership, and instruction. Additionally, McDowell has several years of teaching experience in middle and high school science and mathematics.

McDowell serves as the chair of the advisory board for One Percent for Education, facilitating leading experts in shaping a national narrative for advancing public education. Additionally, McDowell serves on the School of Environmental Leadership board, tasked with scaling innovation in secondary school environments. McDowell teaches graduate courses at San Francisco State University to aspiring educational leaders. McDowell is the CEO of Hinge Education, LLC, supporting professional learning in educational systems around the world. He is an international presenter, speaking on instruction, learning, leadership, and innovation. He is a consultant, providing services in problem- and project-based learning, teaching and learning, and systems and site leadership. He is the author of *Rigorous PBL by Design: Three Shifts for Developing Confident and Competent Learners* (2017); *The Lead Learner: Improving Clarity, Coherence, and Capacity for All* (2018); and *Developing Expert Learners: A Roadmap for Growing Confident and Competent Students* (2019).

He holds a bachelor's degree and a master's degree from the University of Redlands and a doctorate in education from the University of La Verne. McDowell and his wife, Quinn, live in Northern California with their two children, Harper and Asher.

To book Michael McDowell for professional development, contact pd@Solution Tree.com.

FOREWORD

by Jay McTighe

I am writing this foreword in the midst of the COVID-19 pandemic. This extraordinarily disruptive occurrence has resulted in hundreds of thousands of deaths and caused economic turmoil worldwide. Despite the mayhem it has wreaked, the pandemic offers an instructive lesson to educators—namely, that we are educating today's students for an increasingly complex, interconnected, and unpredictable world. No longer will success be determined by who can remember the most. A modern education needs to place a premium on transfer, and McDowell makes this case. Indeed, developing students' abilities to apply their learning to new, even unimaginable, situations should be considered the new basic skill. Yet the devil is in the details. What exactly does it mean to teach for transfer and real-world application?

McDowell begins to answer this question by highlighting a trio of interrelated goals: (1) developing foundational knowledge and basic skills; (2) helping learners achieve deep learning of underlying concepts and processes of the disciplines; and (3) cultivating the cross-disciplinary skills (for example, critical thinking, creativity, and self-directed learning) needed for addressing real-world challenges and opportunities. He then employs a worthy analogy to highlight the differences between working in an office and working in a garage. The office describes more traditional schooling in which students acquire the basics and then develop deeper disciplinary understandings, whereas the garage is the home of the inventors who seek to apply their learning to tackle complex issues and problems using 21st century skills that traverse content domains.

McDowell's approach is sound, especially since he thoughtfully threads the needle between two prevailing camps—the advocates of transdisciplinary 21st century skills via project-based learning contrasted with those who declare that substantive content knowledge is requisite. As is the case with most educational pendulum swings, the optimal approach lies somewhere in the middle.

The book is scholarly without being ivory tower, practical without being simplistic. The author cites relevant research with the assurance of an academic, while offering practical advice with the clarity and confidence of a veteran educator. Using a variety of diverse examples and illustrative frameworks, he describes ways to prioritize and focus teaching around the big ideas of the disciplines. Then he illustrates the process of transitioning students to authentic applications within the wider world beyond the school.

As a grandfather, I think carefully about the type of schooling that I want for my one-, two-, and five-year-old grandchildren. McDowell's book captures my vision and hope. It deserves a careful read.

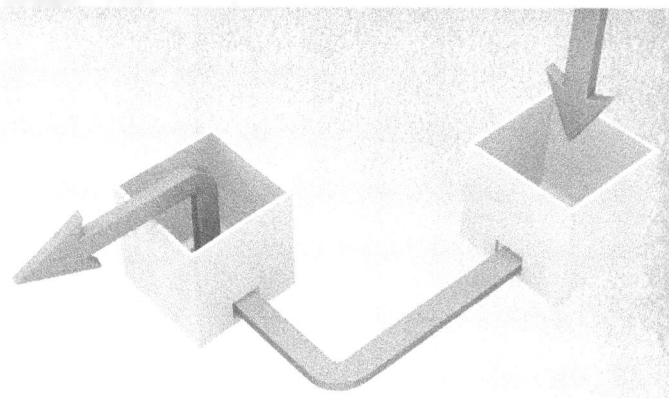

Finding Our Focus

*Experts head off to their corner offices and lecture halls. The garage
is the space for the hacker, the tinkerer, the maker. The garage is not
defined by a single industry; instead, it is defined by the eclectic interests
of its inhabitants. It is a space where intellectual networks converge.*

—STEVEN JOHNSON

n early 2001, I conducted medicinal-plant research as part of a study-abroad program in Kenya, and a core part of my work was to study the loss of certain plant
species that local residents used as forms of primary health care. During this time,
I attended classes in which I learned about line transects, a method for estimating
the distribution of organisms in an area; ways to identify medicinal plants; and ail-
ments that medicinal plants addressed, such as malaria and toothaches. The manner
in which I was taught and expected to learn this information was similar to almost
all the experiences I'd had when I was a young student in school. I was in a classroom and received direct input from a teacher, who gave me time to practice, both
with feedback and independently, and usually some sort of grade to reflect my level
of proficiency. Everything was fairly routine.

After collecting and reviewing a significant amount of data on plant distribution,
I learned that the number of medicinal plants was declining at a significant rate and
that, within a few years, the plants would no longer be available. I was determined
to present solutions to conserve the plants for the local community, who needed
these resources. However, over the next several days, a series of circumstances illustrated to me that the problem and its solution were not as routine as I had originally
assumed. The experience would be emblematic of the rest of my work experience:
the classroom is a routine place—the broader world and the problems therein are
anything but.

First, I had an opportunity to meet with a Maasai elder, who asked about my
work and recommendations. He listened intently, paraphrasing my statements and

posing questions. Finally, he asked me, "Have you thought about asking the local residents what they think the problem is and what solutions they may have?" I felt a sense of shame in that I'd neglected to ask for and appreciate others' perspectives. Immediately, I began seeking community members' views on the chief problem, and I inquired about what they saw as emerging problems and what solutions they would propose.

Second, as I developed a solution to the problem, a mentor from miles away suggested that I explore other fields of study and analyze common issues, approaches to decision making, and methods for problem solving. I had never thought about solving a biology problem outside the sciences, so I began scanning economics articles pertaining to the challenges of unregulated markets, evaluating the marketing field and understanding how we influence others, and reflecting on novels such as *Ishmael* and *The Story of B*. I homed in on fields different from those I had studied, looking for odds and ends that together would create a better solution.

Finally, before I presented my proposal to my professors, the national government had made significant changes to policies that impacted the financial resources available in the areas of plant conservation, tourism, and farming. This was, after all, two months after 9/11, and change was a constant.

By incorporating others' perspectives, sampling various disciplines, and adjusting to account for unexpected changes, I developed more-viable proposals that were considered for implementation in the local context. This formative experience fundamentally changed the way I thought about learning and teaching. Over the next several years, I worked to integrate the idea that students need to not only learn facts and ideas but also cultivate knowledge and skills to look broadly across fields, experience different perspectives, and handle sudden changes. In other words, in my classroom, I worked to find ways to teach students the depth of my subject area and the necessary breadth of reaching outside the field to apply or transfer knowledge to answer real-world problems. This is the key reason I wrote this book—to support K–12 teachers in learning practical ways to develop transfer-level work in the classroom.

A metaphor that resonates for me and may be helpful for teachers when working toward balancing breadth and depth is to give students the experiences of the office and the garage, spaces that science author Steven Johnson (2014) describes in *How We Got to Now: Six Innovations That Made the Modern World*. The office—the place where we learn facts and skills and gain an in-depth understanding of a discipline— is critical but incomplete. The office is a kind of environment in which students engage in clear, routine tasks; receive feedback directly from teachers; and gauge progress with daily lightbulb moments.

But students also need the garage—an emblem of the innovator's workspace, which exists outside the traditional spaces of work and research. In the garage, peripheral interests and broad, cross-subject thinking have the room to grow and evolve.

Moreover, the garage is where we face what journalist David Epstein (2019) refers to as "wicked problems" (p. 213). This is a place where "the rules of the game are often unclear or incomplete, there may or may not be repetitive patterns and they may not be obvious, and feedback is often delayed, inaccurate, or both" (Epstein, 2019, p. 21). The garage feels like the ultimate anti–lightbulb moment; it's filled with new challenges, new ideas, and new perspectives that complicate the original problem—make it much more unwieldy than we anticipated.

When I was in Kenya learning about line transects, I had several lightbulb moments. There, I was in the office, which presented *kind* problems to me. When I listened to others' observations about the medicinal-plant problem, looked to other fields, and incorporated the dynamics of the local context, I knew that I had left the office and ventured into the garage, which required me to use new tools and think differently.

Figure I.1 illustrates the types of learning experiences I design for my students. The person on the left represents the student who is developing depth in learning. This student spends a significant amount of time learning the core components of a discipline. The student on the right is developing the knowledge and skills of breadth.

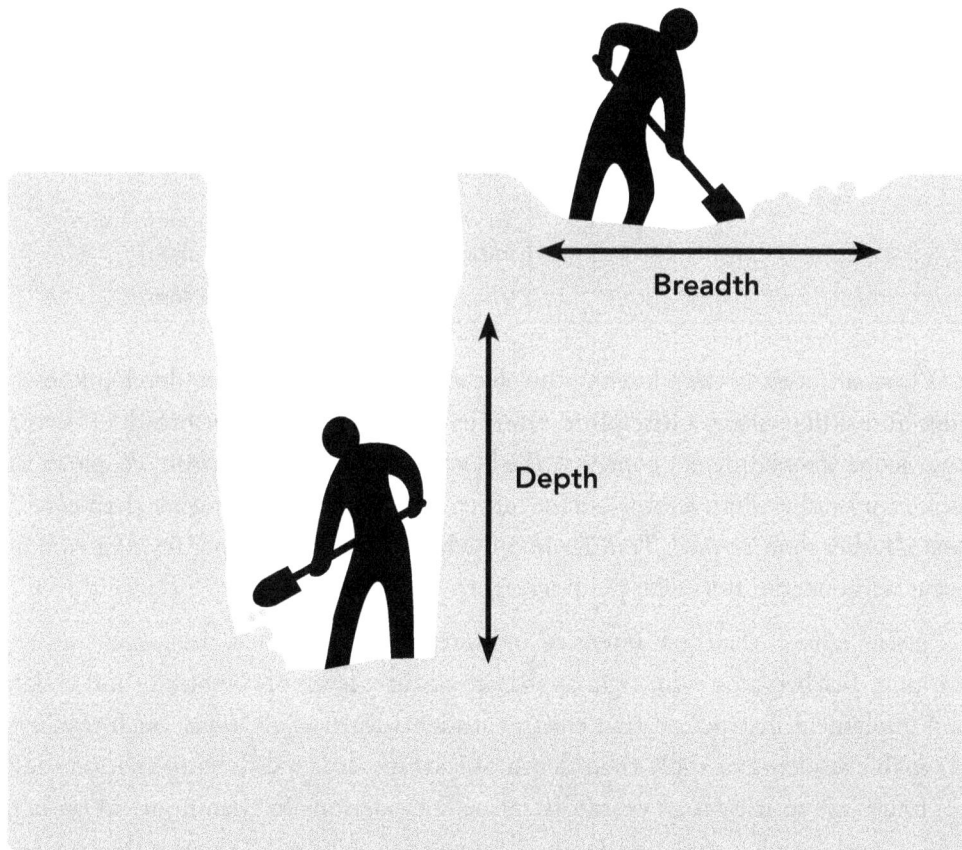

Figure I.1: Depth and breadth of learning.

Depth and breadth relate directly to the terms I use throughout the book to describe the levels of complexity in learning: *surface*, *deep*, and *transfer* (see table I.1). Depth involves the ability to understand core ideas and to relate those ideas, or to possess surface and deep knowledge and skills. Breadth involves the ability to apply those ideas across disciplines to new contexts—to possess transfer knowledge and skills.

Table I.1: Levels of Complexity

Level of Complexity	Description	Answers the Following Questions
Surface	I can define and label ideas and use skills, but I can't connect the ideas and skills together.	What are the key attributes or ideas that I need to understand? What are the key skills? How do I solve this problem?
Deep	I can relate ideas and connect skills, but I can't apply the ideas and skills to different situations.	How do these ideas relate? Why do we solve problems using a certain strategy? Why is this the most efficient or effective method?
Transfer	I can apply ideas and skills to different situations.	When and where do these ideas and skills apply—and under what conditions? Should we employ certain strategies in this situation? To what extent are we missing additional information to solve this problem? Who is impacted by this problem?

Where surface and deep learning involve a narrowing of focus to develop knowledge and skills within a discipline, transfer learning is all about breadth—using knowledge across different contexts. The key to transfer is comparison. People must look *across* rather than *within*—*wide* rather than *narrow*, *open* rather than *closed*, *lateral* rather than *vertical*. Transfer is at the heart of this book, but transfer cannot occur without educators who promote rigor.

I define *rigor* as the equal intensity and integration of surface, deep, and transfer learning. Teachers who value rigor appreciate all three levels of complexity and design and implement instruction that ensures students learn at all levels. Such teachers (1) enable students to apply their depth of learning across different situations and (2) find ways to use broad cross-discipline comparisons to then home in on one subject and enrich a student's depth of knowledge. Figure I.2 depicts the concept of rigor.

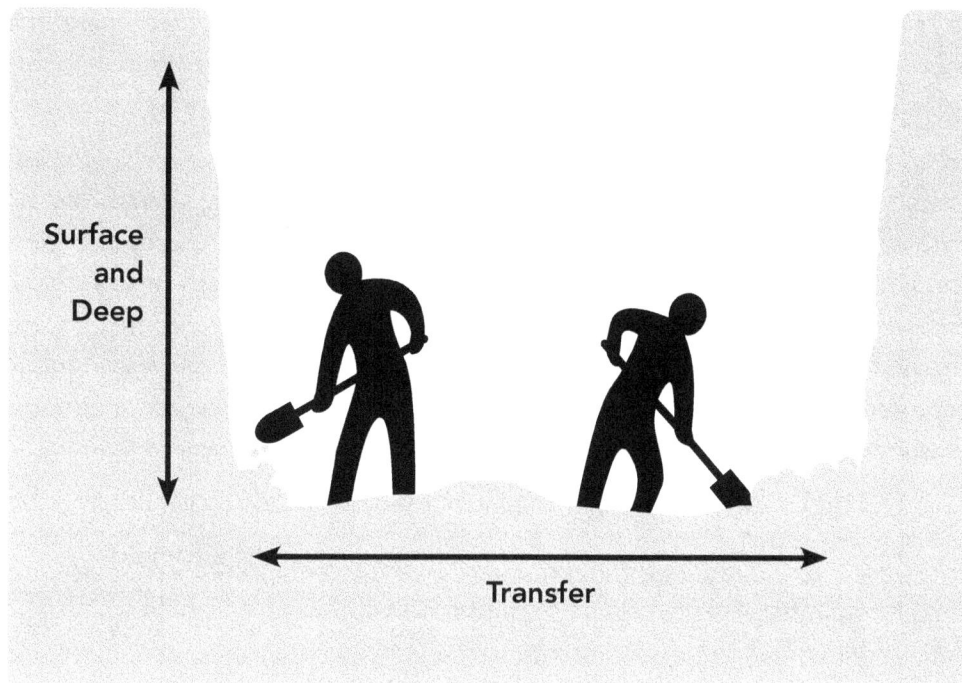

Figure I.2: Representation of rigor.

Since my time in Kenya, I have taught a number of students with the intention of having them learn high school mathematics, biology, and environmental science, while providing them with challenging problems that intersect government, economics, English language arts, physical education, and chemistry. Moreover, my goal has been to equip students with the tools that enable them to navigate the office and the garage. Such tools prepare students to handle setbacks, face ambiguity, and collaborate with others. When students can work in the office *and* the garage, or combine the elements of depth and breadth in learning, they develop innovative expertise—that is, the ability to not only know subjects deeply but solve real-world problems across various disciplines and contexts.

This book offers a framework that has enabled my students—and those of a number of teachers around the world—to innovate, solve challenging real-world problems, and develop expertise. Before we explore it, I'd like to further define *transfer* and what I mean by *teaching for transfer*, discuss the structure of the book and how to approach it, explain what you can achieve by following the book's framework, and talk about your toolbox for designing rigorous learning.

Transfer Defined

Educational consultant and author Jay McTighe (2018) argues that educators' ultimate long-term goal is ensuring that students transfer their learning. Renowned developmental psychologist Howard Gardner (1999) defines *transfer* as an individual's ability to appropriately apply a concept, skill, or theory within a domain of knowledge to a new context; this is foundational for the definition in this book. However, there is more to this term.

McTighe (2018) writes that generalized skills such as collaboration, problem solving, decision making, and critical thinking are indispensable in transfer-level learning. Education scholars Amina Youssef-Shalala, Paul Ayres, Carina Schubert, and John Sweller (2014) add that the development and employment of surface- and deep-level knowledge and skills are essential for transfer to occur. In addition, Epstein (2019) argues that people who can separate contexts from the deeper underlying structure of a problem are those most likely to solve problems across different situations—and thus transfer. So transfer learning requires a student to have:

▸ Problem-solving strategies to address a problem or meet a challenge

▸ Surface and deep knowledge and skills in an academic discipline

▸ Knowledge of the context or contexts in which content should be applied

Figure I.3 illuminates the primary aspects of transfer learning: surface and deep knowledge and skills, context knowledge, and problem-solving approaches.

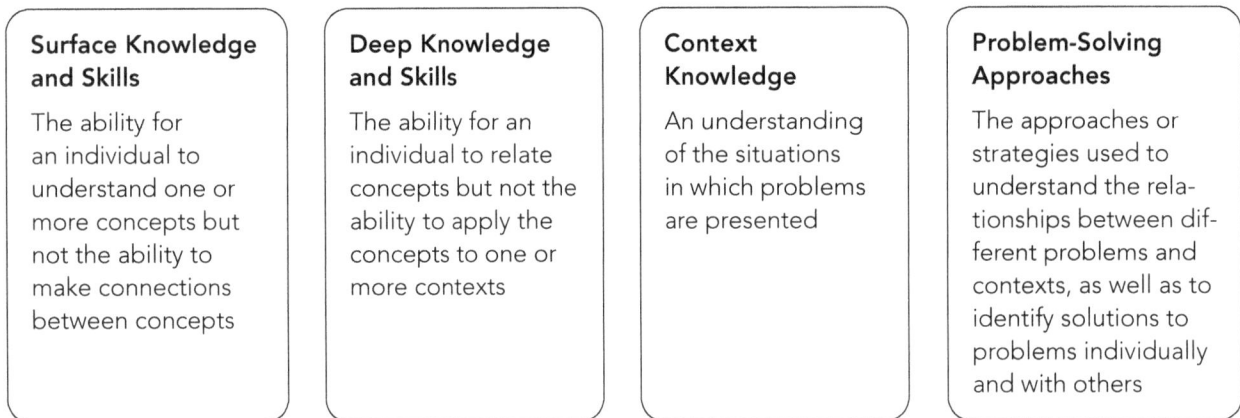

Surface Knowledge and Skills	**Deep Knowledge and Skills**	**Context Knowledge**	**Problem-Solving Approaches**
The ability for an individual to understand one or more concepts but not the ability to make connections between concepts	The ability for an individual to relate concepts but not the ability to apply the concepts to one or more contexts	An understanding of the situations in which problems are presented	The approaches or strategies used to understand the relationships between different problems and contexts, as well as to identify solutions to problems individually and with others

Figure I.3: Components of transfer learning.

Our work, then, as teachers is to combine these elements that enable students to develop their knowledge and skills to transfer. Let's look at an example of transfer-level work in the classroom. Figure I.4 provides a visual of the types of learning students are engaged in at the surface, deep, and transfer levels. At the top of the figure, two separate circles represent two separate ideas at the surface level. Here, students are developing an understanding of ideas but are unable to relate the ideas. They may understand what food chains and food webs are, but they don't necessarily see the relationship between the two constructs, why the constructs are important to understand, and when and where such concepts apply in real life. As students move to a deeper level of understanding, illustrated by the overlapping circles in the middle configuration, they begin to relate the ideas of food chains and food webs and understand the deeper principles of biology (for example, the movement of energy in an ecosystem). They grasp the connection between multiple ideas.

Next, students relate these deeper principles to different contexts to solve a problem (for example, the increase of domoic acid in seals and sea lions in Northern California, the rise in kiwi bird deaths due to the introduction of ferrets in New Zealand, and the decline in golden eagle populations due to the installment of wind turbines). Here, the two opaque overlapping circles indicate a student's ability to understand the connection between different contexts. Students spend time examining each context and how the key principle of energy movement in an ecosystem plays out when direct and indirect human impact manipulates ecosystems.

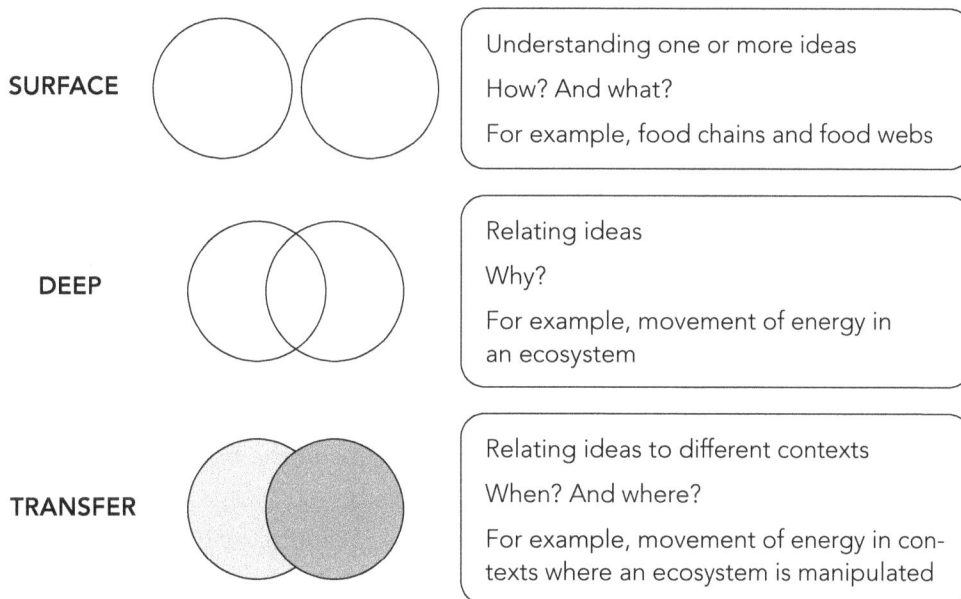

SURFACE

Understanding one or more ideas

How? And what?

For example, food chains and food webs

DEEP

Relating ideas

Why?

For example, movement of energy in an ecosystem

TRANSFER

Relating ideas to different contexts

When? And where?

For example, movement of energy in contexts where an ecosystem is manipulated

Figure I.4: Example of transfer-level work.

Transfer tasks vary in terms of their degree of difficulty. For example, students transferring their understanding of the Apple iPhone to the Samsung Galaxy would be applying a lesser degree of transfer than transferring their understanding of parametric statistics to a challenge in the social sciences (for example, using data to influence voters in the next election) or biology (for example, using data to influence federal and state approaches to flatten the curve during a pandemic). Because teachers must determine the level of difficulty they expect for students within each unit of study, this book will look at the following levels of transfer.

> ▸ **Near transfer:** Applying knowledge within one subject to one context related to the subject (for example, relating food chains to the rise of kiwi deaths in New Zealand)

> ▸ **Near-to-far transfer:** Applying knowledge within one subject to more than one context related to the subject (for example, analyzing the increase of domoic acid in seals and sea lions in Northern California, the rise in kiwi deaths due to the introduction of ferrets in New Zealand, and the decline in golden eagle populations due to the installment of wind turbines)
>
> ▸ **Far transfer:** Applying knowledge across multiple subjects to different contexts (for example, examining the sociopolitical realities and biological impact of a decline in certain populations, interviewing people within the local context, and using statistical analysis to forecast potential changes in populations given specific assumptions and solutions)

What It Means to Teach for Transfer

As we will see throughout this book, teaching for transfer is much more effective when we don't attempt to teach to this level of complexity in the manner that we do for surface and deep learning. Transfer requires specific teaching strategies that enable students to compare and contrast different contexts, connect surface and deep knowledge to the relationship between contexts, and leverage problem-solving strategies to address challenges.

As Johnson (2010) states:

> It is not so much a question of thinking outside the box, as it is allowing the mind to move through multiple boxes. That movement from box to box forces the mind to approach intellectual road-blocks from new angles, or to borrow the tools from one discipline to solve problems in another. (p. 173)

Often, we think of innovation as big, bold, "ahead of our time" dreams—that is, outside the box—when in fact innovation is the collision of ideas across different fields, the gradually occurring hunches that colleagues debate and test, and the small shifts that we make in things we already know. This is not incrementalism in the case of refining a strategy or improving a slight variation in a solution but rather reimagining strategies and solutions by putting together ideas in a different way. This is the focus we as educators must place in our practice when approaching transfer with students—linking box to box rather than attempting to force students to think outside the box.

Here, we need to enable students to think laterally, and this is where transfer-driven methodologies such as project- and problem-based learning, which are often designed and delivered in one specific context, could be retooled to think across contexts and disciplines to enable students to transfer (McDowell, 2017). Regardless of whether these methodologies are utilized, this book offers specific strategies that teachers may employ in their classroom to ensure students learn surface, deep, and transfer knowledge and skills.

About This Book

The key goal of this book is to substantially impact two components of student learning: (1) *expertise*, a student's knowledge and skills at surface, deep, and transfer levels, and (2) *efficacy*, a student's knowledge and skills in clarifying and acting on learning expectations, handling setbacks and facing challenging problems, and collaborating with others. Our central driving questions, then, are, How do we improve students' expertise? How might we support students in developing efficacy? and Ultimately, in what ways can we ensure students address meaningful real-world problems?

The book is organized around the following six goals of teaching for transfer that enable you to answer these driving questions and help students meet established learning outcomes.

1. **Core learning outcomes:** Teachers ensure students develop surface and deep knowledge of and skills in curricular materials.

2. **Co-construction of expectations:** Teachers involve students in clarifying learning expectations.

3. **Change in the learning experience:** Teachers incorporate change in context, task, perspective, and success criteria to challenge students.

4. **Comparisons across problems:** Teachers engage students in comparing problems and solutions to enable transfer of knowledge and skills across contexts.

5. **Community engagement:** Teachers provide students with opportunities to engage in real-world experiences to solve transfer-level problems.

6. **Conditions for learning:** Teachers create the right conditions for students to conduct transfer-level work.

Because these goals do not exist in isolation, they are interwoven throughout the book, with each chapter focusing on one or more goals. To ensure these goals are easy to implement in practice, each of the chapters offers a variety of research-based practices, classroom-tested tools, real-life examples, and accessible tables, checklists, rubrics, and protocols.

Chapter 1 sets the foundation for ensuring students meet surface- and deep-level learning outcomes they need to effectively access and engage in transfer-level work. Moreover, this initial chapter lays the foundational work of building student efficacy.

This first chapter maps out the classroom as the office space, while the rest of the book provides the outline for transforming the classroom into the garage, where students can tinker.

Chapter 2 shifts to a discussion on transfer. Here, we begin the work in the garage. This chapter focuses on setting the expectations for transfer and the critical need for student involvement in this process.

Chapter 3 delves into the idea that transfer knowledge and skills require students to face the reality of change and instability that experts often encounter in their own work. For example, in an immersive unit of study in high school government and economics, students might encounter sudden national policy changes, such as the introduction of tariffs and the defunding of space exploration—the sorts of unplanned variables that play into an expert's ability to understand and solve problems. These changes make the transfer-level problems and work more realistic for students and reinforce surface and deep knowledge, ultimately enhancing students' expertise and efficacy over time.

Chapter 4 focuses on developing students' ability to learn how to compare problems within and across contexts, as well as engage with people outside the classroom to better understand problems. Together, these skills empower students to effectively address near-, near-to-far-, and far-transfer problems.

Finally, chapter 5 provides resources and tools you can use to implement teaching-for-transfer work in your classroom. This chapter offers steps on how to create a scope and sequence for learning experiences conducted throughout the year and the means for developing and evaluating products, portfolios, and performances with other teachers.

Each chapter closes with reflection questions and next steps, which will assist you in thinking about how the chapter's recommended strategies apply to your own teaching practices and encourage you to make changes and improvements based on the chapter's content.

Figure I.5 offers success criteria for teachers and students to meet the outcomes of developing student expertise and efficacy. You may wish to use it as a checklist when you're designing and implementing a unit of study with your students. But it also serves as a resource for you as you make your way through this book; refer back to it, and check off what you master along the way. Because this is a checklist for the entire book, currently you may be unfamiliar with many of the terms. As you progress through the book, you will become more acquainted with the concepts recorded here.

Goals	Student Success Criteria	Teacher Success Criteria
Core Learning Outcomes Students interact with expertise- and efficacy-based strategies to ensure they acquire surface-, deep-, and transfer-level knowledge, as well as cultivate the skills to take control over their own learning.	Students engage in learning the core knowledge and skills for transfer through the following. ☐ Receiving instruction and teacher feedback that are specifically scaffolded for surface, deep, and transfer learning ☐ Applying strategies to develop efficacy in their own learning	Effective teaching strategies include the following. ☐ Developing lessons that align to high-impact feedback and instructional strategies at surface, deep, and transfer levels ☐ Using strategies that enable students to develop efficacy-based skills in orientation, activation, and collaboration ☐ Designing units of study that engage students at surface, deep, and transfer levels
Co-Construction of Expectations Students interact with teachers, peers, and others outside the school to attain clarity of learning expectations, address transfer problems, and develop strategies that will ensure effective feedback and enable collaboration to solve problems.	Students establish clarity of learning and problem contexts through the following. ☐ Unpacking multiple contexts to derive learning intentions and success criteria ☐ Engaging in inquiry activities to develop purposeful transfer-level challenges ☐ Using cues to identify incomplete or inaccurate knowledge and key questions at surface, deep, and transfer levels, and planning for next steps	Effective teaching strategies include the following. ☐ Co-constructing success criteria with students using multiple examples of levels of success across multiple contexts ☐ Co-constructing driving questions with students across multiple contexts ☐ Establishing routines to test prior knowledge and co-constructing with students the next steps across levels of complexity
Change in the Learning Experience Students face varied dynamics through the learning process to enhance transfer learning and mimic real-world challenges.	Students encounter changes in the following. ☐ Perspectives within the transfer challenge ☐ Task structure or task expectations ☐ Success criteria ☐ Contexts	Effective teaching strategies include the following. ☐ Introducing a variety of perspectives within the transfer challenge ☐ Switching the task structure or augmenting task expectations during a unit of study ☐ Opening up success criteria ☐ Bringing in different tools and rules within the success criteria ☐ Incorporating new contexts before, during, or after the unit of study

Figure I.5: Student and teacher success criteria for the six goals of teaching for transfer.

continued →

Goals	Student Success Criteria	Teacher Success Criteria
Comparisons Across Problems Students develop transfer-level skills to engage in transfer-level problems.	Students engage in transfer-level learning by applying their content knowledge and skills through the following. ☐ Creating analogous problems ☐ Interacting with comparison tasks and contexts ☐ Generating and testing hypotheses	Effective teaching strategies include teaching transfer through the following. ☐ Presenting analogous situations to students ☐ Providing tools, resources, and instruction that enable students to recognize patterns in and across problems ☐ Providing tools, resources, and instruction that enable students to recognize similarities and differences in problems ☐ Providing tools, resources, and instruction that enable students to act on problems
Community Engagement Students solve transfer-level problems by working with people in and out of the classroom.	Students solve transfer-level problems through the following. ☐ Engaging with communities, audiences, and experts in problem contexts ☐ Engaging in problem-solving processes and protocols to generate solutions to the transfer-level problems	Effective teaching strategies include teaching transfer through the following. ☐ Creating situations that require students to collect information from other sources ☐ Providing tools, resources, and explicit instruction that enable students to analyze information from other sources ☐ Providing tools, resources, and explicit instruction to problem solve with others to generate solutions to transfer-level problems
Conditions for Learning Teachers plan for teaching for transfer and ensure that they and students inspect impact on learning along the way.	Students engage in transfer-level problems through the following. ☐ Participating in learning experiences throughout the year that integrate all levels of complexity ☐ Participating in learning experiences throughout the year that integrate orientation, activation, and collaboration ☐ Creating products, portfolios, and performances ☐ Taking part in units of study that follow multiple pathways for meeting surface, deep, and transfer learning	Effective teaching strategies to ensure transfer include the following. ☐ Prioritizing the core curriculum standards ☐ Developing pathways for students to learn surface, deep, and transfer knowledge and skills ☐ Designing open-ended tasks that enable students to demonstrate transfer-level knowledge and skills ☐ Working in teacher teams to enhance student performance and create transfer-level curriculum, instruction, and assessment ☐ Planning structured protocols to support students in interactions with others

*Visit **go.SolutionTree.com/instruction** for a free reproducible version of this figure.*

How to Approach This Book

As shared earlier, this book is designed to support elementary and secondary school teachers by providing practical ways of developing and implementing transfer-level work in the classroom. In addition, through extensive research, reflection questions, and discussions around teacher teaming, this book provides guidance for teacher coaches, professional learning community leaders, and administrators. Because of this broad audience, consider the following four items when using this resource.

1. Transfer-level skills are only impactful when students possess substantial content knowledge acquired through surface and deep learning. This book provides several examples to highlight transfer but may seem somewhat content heavy to elementary teachers, who teach a broad curriculum. While the main text features some elementary examples, refer to the appendices, both in the book and online at **go.SolutionTree.com/instruction**, for additional examples befitting the elementary classroom.

2. Given the book's relatively broad audience—who will have different needs, levels of background knowledge on transfer, and so on—the robust appendices provide concrete practical examples of many of the concepts and strategies referenced in the text.

3. If you are working alone, in order to best enable far transfer, take the time to explore the content standards and curriculum expectations of disciplines that are potentially outside your areas of expertise. This is how you'll best support students in applying surface and deep knowledge in different disciplines to the problem or challenge you propose.

4. Progressive pedagogy is a popular approach to ensuring students experience transfer-level learning, and as such, this book is a helpful guide in ensuring that such pedagogies and assessment schemes are effective in propelling student learning. However, this book does not spend much time discussing problem- and project-based learning and standards-based grading.

The Road Ahead

Educators often pose the dichotomous question, Do we focus on surface and deep learning or transfer learning? John Hattie claims that 90 percent of teaching around the world is geared toward surface learning (personal communication, July 10, 2018). He further argues that it is a rarity for students to engage in deep-learning opportunities unless their teachers have significant expertise in teaching to such levels. In a small percentage of schools, transfer is the core focus, yet such schools may also devalue surface-level learning, resulting in impoverished deep learning.

The tension between surface and deep learning versus transfer learning is real in contemporary schools and plays out in countless classrooms and workspaces around the world. Often, individuals, departments, schools, or school systems decide to focus on transfer learning and hang out in the garage or to focus on surface and deep learning and stick to office work, where textbooks and pacing guides prepare students for tasks in the cubicle.

Schools may have a number of spaces and programs that offer transfer opportunities, such as a fabrication lab, a technology center, or career-pathway certification. But within the academic wings of the school, you can rest assured that the office space is well intact, filling the minds of students with surface and deep knowledge. Imagine the vocational building of a school being the garage. Here, students tinker, explore, pick up spare parts, and make something new. Think of the main building of a school being the office space, where students work on acquiring knowledge and understanding underlying principles of a specific discipline. Now imagine the breezeway that connects these structures. Students regularly passing through this breezeway optimize their learning, joining together the facts, skills, and spare parts of various academic disciplines to solve complex problems. This book will help you cultivate this type of work among your students.

With this book, you will learn how to do the following.

- ▶ Develop units designed for surface, deep, and transfer learning that maximize your impact on student learning while minimizing the amount of time you need to spend planning so that you can focus your time and energy on developing student expertise.

- ▶ Support students at transfer-level learning by generating questions, creating tasks, and incorporating changes during classroom instruction that move students to advanced levels of understanding.

- ▶ Align teaching practices to ensure students meet core outcomes across surface, deep, and transfer levels of complexity.

Your Toolbox for Designing Surface, Deep, and Transfer Learning

In 1949, the Mann Gulch fire raged in the mountains of Montana (Epstein, 2019). Smoke jumpers were called in to extinguish the fire as quickly as possible. This was considered a routine fire—until it wasn't. The situation shifted from a normal, predictable day at the office to an unpredictable day in the garage. As the forest firefighters worked to put out the fire, the fire jumped across the valley and headed toward the firefighters. The foreman yelled for the men to drop their equipment, but only two of the fifteen firefighters did so; the remaining men kept their tools and perished in the fire, as they were unable to climb the steep terrain with their equipment.

Epstein (2019) writes of the event, "One firefighter stopped fleeing and sat down, exhausted, never having removed his heavy pack" (p. 246).

This same phenomenon happened in Colorado in 1994, when firefighters did not relinquish their tools and died with the heavy weight of their backpacks and chainsaws (Epstein, 2019). As psychologist Karl Weick (as cited in Epstein, 2019) notes, "Dropping one's tools is a proxy for unlearning, for adaptation, for flexibility. . . . It is the very unwillingness of people to drop their tools that turns some of these dramas into tragedies" (p. 246). Interestingly, according to research scientist Richard C. Rothermel (1993), some firefighters engaged in training to address nonroutine situations by learning how and when to drop familiar tools (for example, axes and chainsaws) and how to pick up and use new tools in certain situations (for example, developing safety zones and using fire shelters). They integrated a set of tools akin to a Swiss Army knife to face routine and nonroutine problems.

Like firefighters, educators have a set of tools—routines for the office and, for some, the garage. Many of us have been trained for the predictable world of surface and deep learning and teaching. We are familiar with ensuring students have clear learning goals, as well as the direct modeling, guided practice, and independent practice to meet such outcomes. We have been trained to manage a classroom that resembles the predictable environment of the office. However, we need to have a Swiss Army knife, a tool that prepares us to navigate both the environment of the office and that of the garage. As with firefighters who have received training on adaptation to new situations, we must be comfortable with setting aside old tools, picking up new ones, and developing a level of flexibility for our students' sake—to make certain they understand each discipline and are able to move across disciplines to solve challenging problems.

At the end of each chapter, I'll prompt you to think about the tools you already have and what tools you may need to pick up and use when the right situation presents itself. One way to know whether you are lacking a specific tool is to notice the tension you feel when I offer certain ideas and recommend specific strategies. If you immediately disagree with a recommendation or feel like you are not prepared to engage in a given task, pause and make a note of the tension, and identify what you will do to fully consider the idea before rejecting it as something you are unable to utilize. Moreover, if you feel like you don't have the skills to meet a recommendation, record the steps that would best support you in moving toward proficiency.

Conclusion

The future lives of our students will likely be a blend of the office space and the garage. In other words, to handle the change from efficiency of work to problem solving across multiple contexts, students will be required to use a mixture of surface, deep, and transfer knowledge and possess the skills to be efficacious in their learning.

Interestingly, this is the same work for teachers. We are often retooling our units and lessons while sometimes reinventing entire sections of our courses and approaches to our pedagogy.

This book celebrates the nature of learning and requires each of us to reaffirm that teaching is situational to the needs of learners. While there is no one right model for teaching, consider the six goals (core learning outcomes, co-construction of expectations, change in the learning experience, comparisons across problems, community engagement, and conditions for learning) discussed earlier in this introduction as guides to help you design models or frameworks that work for your circumstances.

There will be practices in this book that you are already implementing, practices about which you have reservations, and practices that may seem to be beyond the scope of reality. Lean into those changes in practice that will potentially improve your efficiency in the office space and expand your ingenuity when you are tinkering in the garage. This will give you the opportunity to experience what your students go through as they progress from novices to experts.

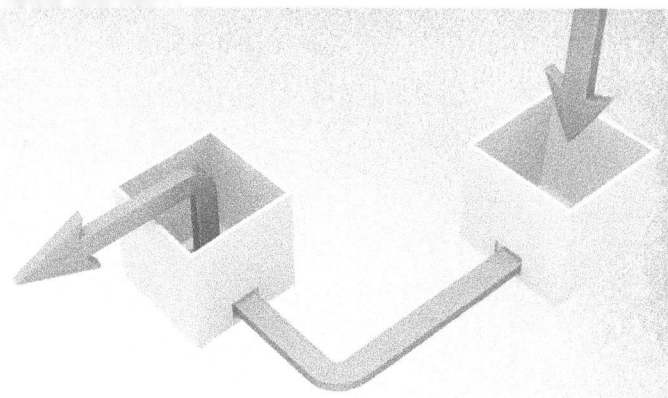

Chapter 1

Laying Foundations:
Building Surface-and-
Deep Networks

*The adjacent possible is a kind of shadow future, hovering
on the edges of the present state of things, a map of all the
ways in which the present can reinvent itself.*

—STEVEN JOHNSON

Our brains are made up of a series of networks, roughly one hundred billion neurons that comprise groups of one thousand or so neurons connecting to one another. Such networks are considered *plastic*, in that neurons can form other configurations. New ideas are based on the formation of a new network of neurons. Our genetics and personal experience shape these neuron groups and groups within groups of neurons (Johnson, 2010). As educators, we have an opportunity to support students in reshaping and reconfiguring these neural networks to become better learners and creators.

Johnson (2010) describes a good idea as a network—a constellation of neurons that work together and form new ideas in our minds. For experts, a good idea is the possibility for a better future—new iterations and changes to the status quo. As Johnson (2010) states, experts have a keen understanding of the "present state of things," or, put simply, they have the foundational knowledge and skills in their discipline (p. 31). They are searching for the "adjacent possible"—ideas and solutions outside the knowledge and skills they already possess to solve problems (Johnson, 2010, p. 31). For learners, a good idea is coming to understand the present state of things. This may include comprehending multiplication facts, comparing connectives when writing, and understanding the devastating impact of genocide on an entire civilization. The question is, How do we build networks that prepare learners for both learning foundational facts and underlying principles of an academic discipline and developing the networks for solving future real-world problems across multiple fields of study? In this chapter, we'll understand the distinction between two types of networks that build expertise and our ability to transfer, and we'll spend time discussing how we can support students in developing the networks associated with foundational knowledge and skills.

Two Systems of Networks

When it comes to developing expertise and our ability to transfer our learning, there are essentially two systems of networks that we want to form in the mind. The first is composed of surface-and-deep-knowledge-and-skills networks, or *surface-and-deep networks*, which are based on developing important ideas that others have already explored and understood. These networks primarily focus on grasping facts, ideas, and procedures (that is, surface learning) and then relating those facts, ideas, and procedures to understand the underlying principles of a discipline (that is, deep learning). The second system of networks is composed of transfer-knowledge-and-skills networks, or *transfer networks*, which are based on the possibilities lurking outside the periphery of what is known. In the 21st century, students need to develop both kinds of networks: those needed to create the next innovation (transfer networks) and those that can maximize the replication and efficiency of such an innovation (surface-and-deep networks).

Understand Surface-and-Deep Networks

Surface-and-deep networks are those that form the basis of expertise. As students build these networks, they develop an understanding of the core knowledge of a discipline, such as science, history, or English language arts. For example, students must be able to understand the similarities and differences between native and nonnative organisms in an ecosystem. The development of surface and deep knowledge is best cultivated by curriculum that is anchored in core content knowledge. Moreover, according to journalist Natalie Wexler (2019) and educational consultant Dylan Wiliam (2018a), the use of traditional instructional methodologies becomes powerful for student learning. Students need to be in the office space, focusing on defining terms such as *invasive*, elaborating on their understanding, and receiving specific direct instruction and targeted feedback. As students move to deep-level learning, they begin reading and discussing the underlying principles of evolution and adaptation and the relationship between those theories and concepts, and native and nonnative species. They build knowledge and develop an enduring understanding of a subject. The surface-and-deep network serves as a precursor for fully accessing and using transfer learning.

Surface-and-deep networks are all about lightbulb moments for novices. Understanding why we find a common denominator when adding fractions or recognizing the strengths and frailties of *To Kill a Mockingbird*'s (Lee, 1960) Atticus Finch when discussing race are immediate eureka moments for students when they understand core ideas. Teachers can often easily anticipate these eureka moments for their students because they know the material, have planned lessons according to expectations, and have conducted timely assessments and adapted instruction to ensure students understand the key objectives of the lesson. Teachers intentionally design the processes necessary to create personal experiences where students build the networks to read stories, write essays, understand conics, and prove theorems.

Reconfigure Surface-and-Deep Networks for Transfer Networks

Whereas surface-and-deep networks are all about core knowledge development, transfer networks are designed for application. Transfer networks take painstaking time to develop and are rarely instantaneous creative breakthroughs but rather fits and starts, networks built through exploring and testing, failing and regressing, showing a mixture of gradual successes, punctuated growth, and at times stagnation and backsliding.

Transfer networks are associated with applying the key ideas of surface and deep learning to new problems and new contexts. These networks require a regrouping of neurons that allows people to connect ideas and solutions from different fields of study and personal experiences to new challenges. Describing the nature of transfer networks, Epstein (2019) offers the term *lateral thinking*, which was "coined in the 1960s for the reimagining of information in new contexts, including the drawing together of seemingly disparate concepts or domains that can give old ideas new uses" (p. 193).

Through his work as the CEO of Design that Matters, Timothy Prestero serves as an excellent example of this lateral thinking—the transfer network at play. In her *New York Times* article "Looking Under the Hood and Seeing an Incubator," journalist Madeline Drexler (2008) explains how Prestero built incubators for the developing world and ensured that the parts used in the incubators were familiar to the residents of remote villages of West Africa, as well as countries such as Nepal and Indonesia, where the incubators would be used. He used spare car parts to build the incubators so that they could easily be fixed by local residents. The solution to developing incubators and identifying an innovative approach to ensure their long-term sustainability was brought about through a foundation of surface and deep knowledge, as well as Prestero's collaborating with experts in technology and medicine and engaging and problem solving with residents of each community (Drexler, 2008).

After the NeoNurture incubator design, Prestero (2012) went further with his design work. He began to look across other fields, including finance, government, manufacturing and distribution, and sociology. This lateral thinking—of moving beyond core knowledge and skills in one domain and scanning various disciplines and contexts to solve real-world problems—led him and his team to mitigate a multitude of real-world problems through their development of different products, including the Firefly, an invention to cure jaundice (Arnolda et al., 2018).

Transfer networks are natural parts of the human system that, according to researchers John Sweller, Jeroen J. G. van Merriënboer, and Fred Paas (2019), "occur automatically and unconsciously without explicit teaching" (p. 271). We naturally "engage in basic social functions, solve unfamiliar problems, transfer previously acquired knowledge to novel situations, make plans for future events that may or may not happen, or regulate our thought processes to correspond to our current environment" (Sweller et al., 2019, p. 270). However, even though we have intrinsically acquired the rudimentary skills to think about and solve problems, we may lack the subject-specific knowledge to utilize those skills effectively in specific discipline areas. Moreover, we lack time to practice and receive feedback to hone our skills in transfer, especially in academic environments.

This is not to say that teachers do not have a role in actively teaching transfer-level skills to students but rather that most teachers have students who are wired to engage in transfer-level work. As such, teachers should leverage students' intrinsic abilities to engage in transfer and then work to refine such abilities over time. The challenge is that the best means to support surface-and-deep networks are not completely aligned to the best way to leverage transfer networks.

Whereas surface-and-deep networks are often associated with understanding and recycling old ideas, transfer networks are related to reconfiguring and rearranging surface and deep knowledge within and across disciplines to find creative ways to solve problems. Often, transfer networks are about finding spare parts from different fields and applying them to new problems. In the teaching and learning process, teachers have an opportunity to develop these two systems of networks by strategically aligning instruction. For example, if we want students to build surface-level knowledge of the various organs and organ systems of the body, then students would be best served by engaging in strategies tied to surface learning. This may include teachers using direct instruction for organ systems, tasking students with creating an outline of the systems, offering mnemonics, and handing out practice tests. As students begin to consolidate this information into a general understanding of homeostasis (that is, deep-level knowledge), teachers may incorporate strategies such as classroom discussion and self- and peer evaluations and feedback. As students move to the lateral thinking that characterizes transfer networks, they begin to address questions such as *To what extent can we prevent children from dying of jaundice?* and *How can our understanding of homeostasis help us make better decisions related to business supply chains during a pandemic?* Here, students need to use their surface and deep knowledge to see and address problems within and across multiple fields to generate solutions. And here, teachers use instructional strategies that allow students to see similarities and differences, recognize patterns in new situations, and participate in far-transfer learning.

Misalignment of our instructional strategies can reduce the development of students' systems of networks over time. The role teachers often play in inquiry-based learning is that of the facilitator designing processes for students to acquire surface and deep knowledge through independent work, self-discovery, or product development with others. As such, they are often not providing significant corrective interventions related to students' learning. Such approaches are inappropriate and ineffective for building surface-and-deep networks. Even during transfer-network construction, teachers must take an active role in enabling students to build their understanding of ideas across various contexts. We should always remember that constructivism is not a theory of teaching but a theory of knowing and developing knowledge (Hattie, 2009).

How, then, do we ensure students have the surface and deep knowledge to effectively develop transfer learning?

How to Help Students Build Surface-and-Deep Networks

Western society has indeed built schools for surface-and-deep-network construction. In fact, as Sweller and colleagues (2019) note, "educational institutions were invented because of our need for people to acquire knowledge" of surface and deep learning (p. 271). We have also built schools that counter the notion of acquiring knowledge and instead focus primarily on leveraging transfer knowledge and skills with methodologies that have a low impact on student learning at surface and deep levels (Hattie, 2009; McDowell, 2017). Though such schools have the potential of making an impact at the transfer level (McDowell, 2018), often they deemphasize strategies such as direct instruction, which, as discussed previously, have a profound impact on surface and deep learning.

Our traditional surface-to-deep-focused systems *and* transfer-focused programs are both lacking in fully rounded educational benefits. Students need a rigorous and relevant program of study that enables them to develop expertise *within* disciplines and experience *across* disciplines. My intention with this book is to explore ways we may effectively develop programs that ensure surface-and-deep and transfer networks flourish for all students, and this chapter focuses primarily on developing a blueprint for the former.

Students often must distinguish between learning goals or intentions, learning contexts, the tasks that need to be accomplished, and the structure of work that is required to perform those tasks. When teachers present students with these pieces of information, students typically struggle with distinguishing what they need to do from what they are learning. Suppose that students walk into the classroom and are given instructions that they need to complete a PowerPoint presentation in groups of four on the role of sea otters in a food chain. The students must then discern what they are learning (food chains) from what they are being asked to complete (PowerPoint), the learning context (sea otters), and the way in which they work (groups of four).

Students may have a difficult time navigating and figuring out these common expectations and activities in the classroom. This lack of clarity is especially apparent with novices, who often focus their attention on the most concrete aspects of expectations. They rely heavily on this information because they possess little background knowledge of the content underlying the context of a problem. Experts, in contrast, are able to rely on extensive prior knowledge and therefore discern the learning intentions outside of tasks, context, and work arrangements.

As such, we should articulate the learning intentions and success criteria to students in ways that separate the concrete details of tasks, context, and work arrangements. Moreover, we should spend our time showing students mastery work of the learning intentions and success criteria in multiple ways and multiple contexts so they do not get fixated on one context or one task. Once students have a clear orientation of learning, we can then teach accordingly, providing a coherent set of instructional and feedback strategies that have a good chance of making an impact on student learning. Finally, we should consider embedding strategies for students to self-monitor their own performance so they develop independence in their learning over time.

To support students in building surface-and-deep networks, follow these four steps.

1. Develop learning intentions and success criteria at the surface and deep levels of complexity.

2. Co-construct success criteria with students using multiple examples of success across multiple contexts.

3. Create lessons that align instruction, feedback, and learning strategies to levels of complexity.

4. Incorporate efficacy-based strategies into classroom instruction.

Anchored to the meta-analysis research conducted by Hattie (2009), as well as Wiliam's (2018b) work in *Embedded Formative Assessment*, the preceding steps can make a substantial impact on developing student learning at both surface and deep levels of complexity. These strategies are built on the critical importance of students' gaining clarity of the learning intentions (Almarode & Vandas, 2018; Hattie & Clarke, 2018), the need for alignment of instruction and a student's level of learning (Marzano, 2017), and educators' ever-pressing desire for students to take full responsibility over their own learning to meet surface-, deep-, and transfer-learning expectations (Hattie, 2009).

Develop Learning Intentions and Success Criteria at the Surface and Deep Levels of Complexity

As we will see in the next chapter, transfer networks are based on a network of ideas reconfigured. But to reconfigure a network, one must first be built. To build surface-and-deep networks, students need to have clear surface and deep learning intentions and established success criteria for those learning intentions.

For students to meet these goals, it is helpful for teachers to plan out the learning intentions and success criteria before they begin the unit and lesson with students. As Grant Wiggins and Jay McTighe (2007) have written many times, we must "begin with the end in mind" (p. 25). That is, we must be absolutely clear of what we expect students to learn and what students need to know to be successful in meeting stated goals.

Figures 1.1 through 1.3 illustrate three examples. When planning, ensure that learning intentions and success criteria do not include context and tasks (McDowell, 2019). This will help students focus on the actual goals of learning and increase their chances of transferring across contexts.

Figure 1.1 provides an example of leveled success criteria in an elementary English language arts unit. Visit **go.SolutionTree.com/instruction** for additional elementary school grade-level examples.

Learning Intention: Design a story involving multiple characters.	
Level of Complexity	**Success Criteria**
Surface	• Recognize how we can tell what a character in a play is thinking or feeling through dialogue and events. • Recite the stages of the hero's journey. • Identify key adjectives for describing actions and feelings.
Deep	• Deconstruct the actions and dialogue of different characters throughout the hero's journey. • Relate a character's dialogue to the stages of the hero's journey.

Figure 1.1: Learning intention and leveled success criteria, elementary example.

Figure 1.2 (page 24) provides an example of leveled success criteria in a middle school science class. See figure A.1 in appendix A (page 129) for a sixth-grade example, and visit **go.SolutionTree.com/instruction** for additional middle school grade-level examples.

Learning Intention: MS-ESS2–4. Apply how the cycling of water through Earth's systems, driven by energy from the sun and the force of gravity, is impacted by and impacts humans.

Level of Complexity	Success Criteria
Surface	• Explain how water continually cycles among land, ocean, and atmosphere via transpiration, evaporation, condensation and crystallization, and precipitation, as well as downhill flows on land. • Explain how global movements of water and water's changes in form are propelled by sunlight and gravity.
Deep	• Model the interrelationship between global water movements and sunlight and gravity.

Source for standard: Adapted from NGSS Lead States, 2013.

Figure 1.2: Learning intention and leveled success criteria, middle school example.

Figure 1.3 provides an example of leveled success criteria in a high school economics class. See figure A.2 in appendix A (page 129) for a tenth-grade example, and visit **go.SolutionTree.com/instruction** for additional high school grade-level examples.

Learning Intention: Design a solution for preventing and/or regulating monopolies.

Level of Complexity	Success Criteria
Surface	• Define *monopoly*. • Define *monopoly power*. • List the sources of monopoly power. • Explain barriers to entry and exit. • Draw and explain monopolist revenue curves. • List the means of limiting monopolies. • Define *natural monopoly*.
Deep	• Calculate profit and revenue maximization from data. • Evaluate profit and revenue maximization as a means for monopolist decision making. • Describe the strengths and challenges of a monopoly. • Compare and contrast monopoly and perfect competition.

Figure 1.3: Learning intention and leveled success criteria, high school example.

Co-Construct Success Criteria With Students Using Multiple Examples of Success Across Multiple Contexts

One of the most powerful ways to ensure clarity of learning intentions is to provide students with ways to see and interact with success up front, when we start to teach.

Teachers often skip or ignore this step, providing rubrics in lieu of examples of success. This may be appropriate for experts, rather than novice students, as they have a high degree of background knowledge and an apt schema for the work they are expected to accomplish. Stated differently, rubrics benefit a person with prerequisite knowledge. However, when a person lacks significant background knowledge, rubrics may give only an abstract notion of expectations. Moreover, we tend to communicate to students how we will assess them without giving them an opportunity to fully understand what success looks like and how they can make sense of varying levels of success. Such a passive approach will likely keep students from having a clear understanding of what's expected of them, accurately evaluating their own performance, improving their own work, and giving sound feedback to others.

In action research work conducted in the Ross School District, the district in which I work, we have found that when students receive rubrics or success criteria in tandem with exemplars, novice students have a better chance of gaining clarity of expectations and can monitor their progress toward success throughout the learning process. Additionally, when students work with peers and the teacher to develop the rubric by analyzing successful examples, they will more likely understand and use success criteria (for example, rubrics) to self-assess and support others in improving their learning. Moreover, by going through these processes, they will have a better chance of ensuring that their self-assessments and their feedback to others will be accurate.

Regardless of whether you provide the rubric or have students participate in developing it, it is incumbent on you to ensure students understand what mastery looks like so they have clear expectations. You can support students in this work by providing the means for them to:

▸ Engage with examples of excellence to clarify learning intentions and success criteria

▸ Interact with examples of excellence in different contexts and with different tasks

▸ Give and receive feedback on examples that have differing levels of complexity

Engage With Examples of Excellence to Clarify Learning Intentions and Success Criteria

The following strategy allows students to begin with the end in mind, working backward from the expectations of work to their current level of understanding. For this to be effective, students must interact with concrete examples of mastery work.

For example, let's imagine the goal set by one teacher is for students to develop a personal narrative. Imagine the teacher begins the unit by having students read an effective narrative and attempt to write down the learning intention and success criteria on a piece of paper. Figure 1.4 illustrates a piece of second-grade student writing that might be used in the co-construction process with students. By having students work backward, teachers may preassess what students already know based on the criteria they generate, and they also provide students with an opportunity to self-assess their level of performance relative to expectations.

A Scary Fishing Trip
by Jody Pittock

"I'm cold! I want to go home!" said my younger brother, Sam. We were ice fishing out on the frozen lake in the middle of January. My dad told him to wait patiently for just a bit longer. My little brother was not the least bit happy with that response. He asked again to go to the warm van, where my mom, aunt, and cousin were having hot chocolate.

My father finally said that he would quickly walk my little brother back to the van. Since I was freezing cold too, I agreed to go with them. My older sister, Polly, wished to stay and fish. My dad gave Polly permission to stay on the ice, and we sprinted back to the van. Ice fishing is Polly's favorite sport in the winter.

No sooner had we gotten back to the van than we heard Polly yelling loudly, "Dad!"

A whole crowd of people swarmed around her, and we could not see what was going on. My father and I ran as fast as we could.

"POLLY!" my dad yelled as we neared where my sister had been fishing. "Polly, are you OK?" he frantically shouted.

I was so scared. "Is she hurt? Did she fall in the water?" I asked.

Then the crowd moved slowly, and my father and I got closer. I could see Polly's bright red fishing rod and Polly, standing tall, with a huge grin on her face! She had caught a record-setting fish!

Source: © 2016 by Reach Associates. Used with permission.

Figure 1.4: Personal narrative exemplar.

Next, let's suppose the teacher gives students the opportunity to share criteria as a class and then sort the criteria into surface- and deep-level knowledge and skills. Surface-level criteria would be discrete skills for writing a personal narrative (for example, includes a beginning, a middle, and an end), whereas deep-level criteria would be how those concepts relate (for example, comparing and contrasting words that connect the beginning, middle, and end). Figure 1.5 illustrates a template you may give to students or use as a poster or electronic document that students may populate.

Category	Surface	Deep
Structure		
Grammar and Punctuation		
Content		
Quality of Work		

Figure 1.5: Generating success criteria.

*Visit **go.SolutionTree.com/instruction** for a free reproducible version of this figure.*

Next, the teacher creates a draft of the success criteria for students to use as they construct personal narratives. Figure 1.6 provides an example of teacher- and student-constructed leveled success criteria.

Personal Narrative Success Criteria		
Area of Focus	**Surface**	**Deep**
Structure	I will: • Identify a beginning, middle, and end • Create a plot • List a set of comparing and contrasting connectives	I will: • Link my plot with a clear sequence of events—beginning, middle, and end • Include a series of comparing and contrasting connectives to support transition from one paragraph or section to another • Include a hook and introduce my characters (including the narrator) and setting • Relate the topic with supporting details and conclusion • Connect the resolution to the problem I started with

Figure 1.6: Finalized success criteria example.

continued →

Area of Focus	Surface	Deep
Grammar and Punctuation	I will: • Use the pronoun *I* • Write in complete sentences • Insert commas and quotation marks when there is dialogue • Open sentences with capital letters and close them with end marks	I will: • Integrate a variety of words that indicate time, such as *first, next, last, before, while, then, finally,* and *after* • Incorporate an assortment of pronouns, verbs and verb tenses, adjectives, and contractions
Content	I will: • Identify several details for my reader to understand my story	I will: • Organize the details into a sequence • Connect details to make a coherent story
Quality of Work	I will: • Have others read my writing to make sure it is legible • Use feedback to make changes to my writing	

Interact With Examples of Excellence in Different Contexts and Different Tasks

To ensure they are clear on expectations, students need to see the expectations of learning in a variety of ways. This may include showing students multiple tasks or multiple contexts in which the success criteria are demonstrated. Alternatively, this may include having students complete work in different contexts or via tasks different from those of the exemplars that were used to support a student's understanding of expectations.

Revisiting figure 1.4 (page 26), let's imagine that students review exemplars written as thrilling stories. After the class identifies the success criteria of the pieces, the teacher tells students that there are many types of personal narratives, including diaries, letters, and poems, and that students will write a personal narrative and use the same criteria to self-monitor their performance and give one another feedback. The catch is that they can compose anything *but* a thrilling story. This strategy enables students to clearly understand the success criteria outside of the context and also greatly reduces the risk of their simply copying others' work. Figure 1.7 illustrates an example of a learning intention and success criteria that could be demonstrated in multiple contexts and tasks.

Learning Intention	Success Criteria	Contexts	Tasks
Persuasion	• The thesis states a personal opinion and identifies the issue. • The argument articulates a potential audience and expresses counterarguments. • Points are supported with multiple sources of research. • The conclusion states a personal opinion and summarizes the thesis.	• Organic lunches: Should we eat organic lunches? • Death penalty: Should the death penalty be legalized in every state? • Weapons: Should we arm teachers? • Invasive species: Should we allow invasive species into our homes?	• Create a podcast. • Make a short film. • Deliver an oral presentation. • Role-play. • Submit a writing sample.

Figure 1.7: Learning intention, success criteria, contexts, and tasks.

Give and Receive Feedback on Examples That Have Differing Levels of Complexity

Students are often more successful in clarifying learning expectations and improving their learning—and nurturing that of others—when they have the right tools to give and receive accurate feedback with one another. One powerful way to do this is to categorize work samples by evaluating the work via success criteria and then discussing potential ways of giving and receiving feedback. When done collectively with the entire class, all students are able to calibrate the key success criteria to look for in the work and the most effective means for giving and receiving feedback. Figure 1.8 shows several examples of student work from prior years that current students rate, categorize, and look to improve. Note that if you wish to share former students' work in such a classroom activity, you'll want to seek permission from those students or their guardians. Alternatively, you could create your own work samples.

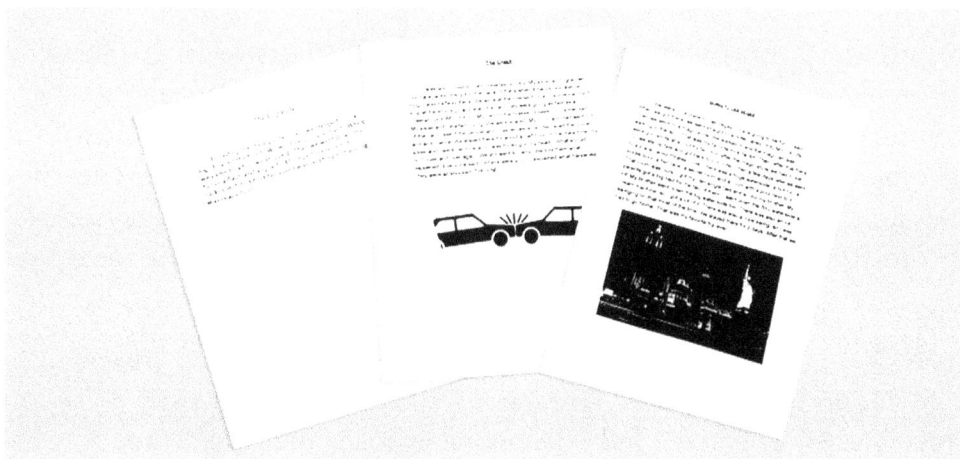

Figure 1.8: Sample student work.

One way to help students ensure accuracy in giving and receiving feedback is to have students publicly practice. Let's go back to our thrilling-story example (see figure 1.4, page 26). Suppose students review this personal narrative, along with other work samples that showcase varying degrees of proficiency and varying contexts (for example, a funny story, a dramatic story, and so forth). The teacher then selects one of the examples and asks students to form groups and evaluate the work based on the success criteria. Students in group A believe that the piece has met all the success criteria. Those in group B believe that some criteria have not been met in the piece of writing. The teacher then asks one student from each group to come to the front of the classroom and explain the group's rationale for each criterion. The other students listen while the teacher asks questions and gives feedback. After this activity, the students draft steps they can take individually to work toward the presented success criteria themselves. When needed, teachers may select one of the work samples and go through their analysis of the piece using the success criteria in front of the entire class. This allows students to see teachers walk through their analysis step by step.

Create Lessons That Align Instruction, Feedback, and Learning Strategies to Levels of Complexity

To support students in moving along the levels of complexity in their work, consider the best instructional approaches to support such learning. The following steps are recommended for lesson planning.

1. Establish routines to test misconceptions and incorrect information.

2. Identify anchor and best-fit strategies for all lessons.

3. Align tasks to surface and deep levels of complexity.

Establish Routines to Test Misconceptions and Incorrect Information

One of the most effective ways to engage students in their learning is to illuminate for them their misconceptions or gaps in knowledge relative to core learning outcomes (Muller, 2008). This helps them clearly understand why they need to learn new material and why previous understandings were incorrect or incomplete. One powerful strategy for supporting students in recognizing their current understanding relative to expectations is to give students their data on a preassessment and ask them to determine their areas of success and growth and to plot out next steps. Related strategies include discrepancy analysis; share, test, and verify; and the error-and-correction process (see figure A.3 in appendix A [page 130] for further details on these strategies).

Identify Anchor and Best-Fit Strategies for All Lessons

To support students in their learning of surface, deep, and transfer, we need to ensure that we anchor our lessons in sound instruction, feedback, and learning strategies. The research has shown that many practices are effective regardless of levels of complexity, whereas others are specific to levels of complexity (Hattie & Donoghue, 2016; Marzano, 2017). Let's call those strategies that are effective across levels of complexity *anchor strategies* and those that are linked to specific levels of complexity *best-fit strategies*. Table 1.1 illustrates a number of strategies that teachers may consider when developing a lesson.

Table 1.1: Anchor and Best-Fit Strategies

Anchor Strategies Effective strategies for enhancing student learning at all levels of complexity	**Student-teacher relationships**—Teachers ensure that students have a safe and respectful environment and that all students know that teachers care about them personally and will do what it takes to ensure they get more than one year's academic growth in one school year. **Assessment-capable learners**—Teachers ensure that students can answer the following questions in class: Where am I going in my learning? Where am I now? What's next? **Teacher clarity**—Teachers ensure that students are clear on the learning expectations of the class, unit, and lesson. **Formative evaluation**—Teachers ensure that they and their students inspect their impact on learning and then take action to improve.		
Level of Complexity	**Surface**	**Deep**	**Transfer**
Definition	Understand one concept, idea, or skill	Understand how concepts, ideas, and skills relate	Understand how to transfer concepts and relationships between concepts to various contexts
Best-Fit Feedback Strategies Effective forms of feedback to enable students to move forward in their learning	As a means to acquire surface-level knowledge: • Teachers and students prompt students to distinguish between correct and incorrect information • Teachers and students prompt students to elaborate on information • Teachers and students redirect students to paraphrase and offer examples	As a means to understand and develop deep understanding: • Teachers and students prompt students to detect errors in solutions • Teachers and students prompt students to articulate similarities and differences in concepts • Teachers and students prompt students to solve problems in multiple ways	As a means to transfer learning to other situations: • Students self-monitor and invest in seeking and acting on feedback to improve • Students evaluate similarities and differences between problems

continued →

Level of Complexity	Surface	Deep	Transfer
Best-Fit Learning Strategies Effective strategies students may use to assist them in their own learning	As a means to acquire information: • Outline • Use mnemonics • Summarize • Underline and highlight • Take notes • Engage in deliberate practice • Rehearse	As a means to connect information: • Seek help from peers • Participate in classroom discussions • Evaluate and reflect • Self-talk and self-question • Use metacognitive strategies	As a means to apply information: • Identify similarities and differences in problems • See patterns in new situations
Best-Fit Instructional Strategies Effective teaching strategies to enable students to develop understanding of core knowledge or skills	As a means to enable students to build surface knowledge and skills: • Use direct instruction • Use a Know, Want to Know, Learned (KWL) chart • Use an advanced organizer	As a means to enable students to build deep knowledge and skills: • Demonstrate with a Venn diagram • Engage in a Socratic seminar • Plan for number talks • Initiate pair-share	As a means to enable students to build transfer knowledge and skills: • Use problem- and project-based learning for far transfer • Introduce a variety of inquiry-based methods

Source: Adapted from McDowell, 2019.

Align Tasks to Surface and Deep Levels of Complexity

As with levels of instruction and feedback, the tasks students are expected to accomplish should match the level of expectations for surface- and deep-level success criteria. Moreover, the most effective tasks are typically those that require substantial levels of reading, writing, and talking.

Table 1.2 illustrates assessment tasks across levels of surface, deep, and transfer learning that involve reading, writing, and talking.

Incorporate Efficacy-Based Strategies Into Classroom Instruction

Students need to develop the knowledge and skills to take full responsibility over their own learning to meet surface, deep, and transfer expectations. This requires students to have knowledge of the learning expectations, their current level of understanding, and the next steps needed to meet outcomes. I refer to this knowledge as *orientation*. Moreover, students need to know the steps required to handle stress, setbacks, and situations that challenge their beliefs, behaviors, and backgrounds. Knowledge of these steps is what I call *activation*. Finally, to take control over their

Table 1.2: Sample Assessment Tasks

Criteria	Sample Assessments
Surface	**Reading:** Preview a passage and highlight key ideas. **Writing:** List and describe key ideas. **Talking:** Recite key ideas.
Deep	**Reading:** Place annotations when key inferences about relationships and principles become apparent. **Writing:** Construct a thesis statement that conveys the relationships of key ideas. **Talking:** Describe the key principles and inferences from a passage.
Transfer	**Reading:** Find other texts that draw on similar inferences and principles within a different context. **Writing:** Write an opinion piece. **Talking:** In front of a panel, argue how the key principles and inferences from the assigned passage relate to a new context.

Source: Adapted from McDowell, 2017.

own learning, they need to know how to give and receive feedback and engage with others on challenging work. This is *collaboration*.

Promote Orientation

I define *orientation* as students' ability to determine the learning expectations in a classroom, as well as their current performance and next steps (McDowell, 2019). The ability to do this is similar to that of swimmers who know the distance they need to swim, their current distance and time, and the immediate strategy they need to take to effectively and efficiently complete their race.

One strategy that supports students in this process is to offer a number of revisions of work samples that align to key success criteria. Figure 1.9 (page 34) illustrates six drafts from a student drawing a butterfly. Note that the learning intention was for the student, Austin, to create a scientific drawing of a butterfly and that the success criteria involved accuracy of shapes and colors.

To support students in focusing on the learning intention and success criteria rather than the context of the butterfly, the teacher tells the students that they may use figure 1.9 as a successful example but they may not create a butterfly. Next, the teacher may:

- Ask students to discuss in pairs how they will give feedback to improve future drafts

- Conduct midlesson stops, inviting students to give feedback on pieces of work that are progressing toward exemplar work

- Have students reflect on performance growth over time

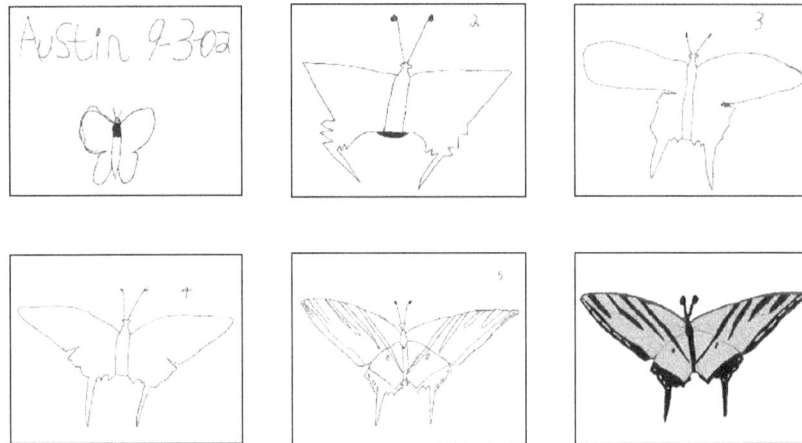

Source: Student artwork by Austin. "Austin's Butterfly." Courtesy of Anser Charter School in Boise, ID, part of the EL Education network. View online at Models of Excellence. http:// modelsofexcellence.eleducation.org/projects/austinsbutterfly-drafts.

Figure 1.9: Austin's butterfly.

See figure A.4 in appendix A (page 131) for an orientation-based-strategy example.

Foster Activation

Activation refers to a student's ability to navigate challenges in the classroom. This takes a both affective and cognitive skill set, as students often face boredom, critical feedback, changes in expectations, and cognitive dissonance that may be uncomfortable.

Two key practices that can help students progress in their learning are as follows.

1. **Focusing forward:** Students determine immediate next steps to improve and resist the urge to ruminate about personal reasons for failing to meet expectations.

2. **Then and now:** Students reflect on strategies that have enabled them to move forward in their learning over time.

Chapter 4 (page 73) discusses the skill of activation at great length as a key element for driving transfer learning. See figure A.4 in appendix A (page 131) for an example of an activation-based strategy.

Facilitate Collaboration

I define *collaboration* as a student's ability to give and receive effective feedback with peers to propel the student's learning and that of others (McDowell, 2019). One of the key leverage points for students to use feedback is peer-to-peer input. Unfortunately, if classroom exercises are not designed correctly, students may give each other inaccurate or inappropriate feedback (McDowell, 2019). For example, if students do not know what success looks like for a personal narrative, then the feedback they give to their peers will be based only on guesswork and prior knowledge of personal narratives. Researcher Graham Nuthall (2007) finds that 80 percent of the feedback students give to and receive from peers in the classroom is incorrect. One key practice teachers can use to ensure accurate feedback is the digging-deeper strategy, described in figure A.4 of appendix A (page 131).

Conclusion

This chapter provided an overview of two systems of networks of the mind, focusing on the surface-and-deep networks that enable students to grasp ideas, as transfer networks in and of themselves are inadequate to solving real-world problems if we do not possess enough core knowledge. Learning to transfer knowledge requires students to have a solid foundation of not only discipline-based ideas and skills but tools to take ownership of their own learning. We walked through a series of steps teachers can take, along with their students, to effectively and intentionally lay this foundation of learning. The next several chapters will build on this base and explore the steps necessary to transfer learning.

Reflection Questions

The following questions are designed for you to address individually or in teams to determine the next steps that you will take in the classroom. When you review these questions, it is important that you reflect on the tools you currently use with students and where you may discover tension between your current beliefs and practices and what I've proposed. If you remember from the introduction, educators usually carry with them a set of tools that work well in certain situations. This chapter's contents may have been somewhat familiar to those teachers who have tools that work well in the office—the classroom focused on surface and deep knowledge and skills. Teachers who come with a set of tools suited to the garage, however, may have found this chapter challenging. Regardless of where you stand, this is an opportunity for you to incorporate new tools.

1. What are the main points that you took away from this chapter?

2. Consider the major steps of the chapter: develop learning intentions and leveled success criteria at the surface and deep levels of complexity; co-construct success criteria with students using multiple examples of success (or levels of success) across multiple contexts; create lessons that align instruction, feedback, and learning strategies to levels of complexity; and incorporate efficacy-based strategies into classroom instruction. What step, or steps, do you feel the most confident about using in your classroom? What step, or steps, do you see as a potential area of growth in your learning and teaching?

3. How will you ensure students develop the skills of orientation, activation, and collaboration?

4. What are your key need-to-knows or questions as you embark on your journey through the next several chapters?

Next Steps

As with the reflection questions, please go through each of these steps individually or as a team and determine what actions you will take in your classroom.

1. Develop a series of learning intentions and success criteria (see figure 1.1, page 23), and review them with other faculty members. One of the best ways to conduct this review is by incorporating a specific protocol for feedback. Consider using the critical-friends protocol, found in figure A.5 of appendix A (page 132).

2. Brainstorm ways to co-develop success criteria with students, and then try the strategies out with students. One way to assess the efficacy of your approach is to ask students the following questions before, during, and after co-construction.

    a. What are the learning intentions?

    b. What does success look like?

    c. How will you know when you have achieved success?

    d. How can you ensure that the feedback you are giving and receiving is accurate?

3. Draft a number of leveled success criteria associated with learning intentions that you think students should learn to transfer. Next, draft a co-construction process to engage students in the learning. Before you launch, receive feedback from other faculty (see the critical-friends protocol in figure A.5 of appendix A, page 132). After the co-construction process, review your work with faculty, keeping in mind the questions that follow.

    a. What successes emerged for you in this process?

    b. What successes emerged for students in this process?

    c. What changes did you notice in your practice from the past?

    d. What changes did you notice in student practice from the past?

    e. How could you improve this process?

    f. What will you do differently going forward?

    g. What should students do differently going forward?

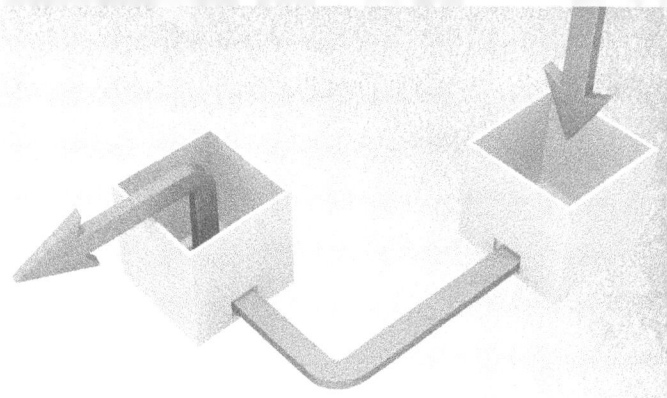

Chapter 2

Moving Beyond Foundations:
Building Transfer Networks

*All decisive events in the history of scientific thought can be described
in terms of mental cross-fertilization between different disciplines.*

—ARTHUR KOESTLER

When we teach students the knowledge and facts they need to build surface-and-deep networks (for example, to solve equations, create lab reports, and understand the branches of government), we are illustrating to them that content is fixed and predictable. If we stick to the script, invest time, and struggle through the central tenets of a discipline, then we will be successful in solving routine problems. Surface-and-deep networks are essential for the work of the office, and if we go further, these networks will eventually allow every student to solve the nonroutine and unpredictable problems of the garage. That is what this chapter is all about—the critical transition from the office to the garage.

As we discussed previously, transfer learning is about lateral thinking and doing. We are looking to find ways to see new connections across academic disciplines and real-world situations to address a new problem. In many ways, this is a question of how we take our knowledge and skills from different fields to make sense of an emerging problem or find a novel solution. Let's look at a few real-life examples of this complex problem solving and, from there, explore the steps we can take in the classroom to help our students build transfer networks.

Director Quentin Tarantino didn't go to film school. He worked at a video store and as such watched a variety of different films, crossed genres, and didn't prescribe to a certain dogma of film but rather integrated many subgenres in his filmmaking. He built a surface-and-deep network through his hours of observing film and simultaneously began orchestrating a transfer network by integrating his work across genres. Tarantino wrote about his thinking related to two of his films—*Pulp Fiction* (1994) and *Django Unchained* (2012):

> I've always been influenced by the spaghetti western. I used to describe *Pulp Fiction* as a rock 'n' roll spaghetti western with the surf music standing in for Ennio Morricone. I don't know if *Django* is a western proper. It's a southern. I'm playing western stories in the genre, but with a southern backdrop. (McGrath, 2012)

Tarantino leveraged his knowledge and skills of film and then used skills of transfer to pick up spare parts from different film and music genres to generate a whole new experience for audiences. He was not *thinking outside the box* but rather connecting multiple boxes—surf music, rock and roll, spaghetti western, and so on—together.

Another example in the arts is film composer Nicholas Britell, who spent part of his life as a trader on Wall Street and, in his spare time, wrote the music that telephone companies play when they put their customers on hold. He found that these very different experiences provided him with the insights he needed to succeed in film. In an interview with Terry Gross (2019), Britell shares that he regularly experiments, engages in deep conversations with directors, notices linkages across musical genres, and works to overlay music that will illustrate the characters' feelings while disrupting the mood of the story. For example, in *If Beale Street Could Talk*, the characters listen to jazz, though Britell made heavy use of strings in the film's score—his way of communicating the themes of love and beauty. His application of disparate musical ideas created a level of depth in the film that someone studying music strictly in the office would not have been able to create. Britell and Tarantino certainly needed to grasp music and movies, respectively, but they needed to diverge—to piece together those odds and ends to create an even better product or solution. In the garage, we tinker. Britell and Tarantino tinker.

There are countless other examples of people who use lateral thinking to collect spare parts from different fields and tinker. Clarence Birdseye, the inventor of TV dinners, and essentially the modern-day frozen-food industry, is one such example. Birdseye spent time fishing with the Inuit. While working on a fishing boat, he saw the waste of rotten cod. This led to efforts in his later work in a fisheries laboratory to reduce waste. Through this combination of experiences, Birdseye created a flash-freezing process that could preserve and maintain the quality of fish (Johnson, 2014).

Other examples of this type of thinking and application abound. Charles Richard Drew invented the first major blood banks, combining refrigeration and his expertise in transfusion. Katharine Blodgett invented nonreflective glass. Both faced trials and tribulations because of race or gender, and both used lateral thinking and tinkered in the garage to innovate. Britell, Tarantino, Birdseye, Drew, and Blodgett did not spend their time in the office refining surface-and-deep networks. Rather, they knew enough from those networks and had unique experiences that allowed for an integration of ideas across various fields. They shifted from the office to the garage. This is how people build transfer networks—engaging in seemingly disparate contexts and finding ideas and solutions between and among them.

How to Help Students Build Transfer Networks

To engage students in developing networks that cross different disciplines, teachers must provide students with scenarios in which they encounter questions, ideas, and content that cross disciplines. The surface-and-deep network is helpful for students in leveraging the key understandings of each discipline, but for transfer learning, students must be able to overlay surface and deep knowledge to address complex interdisciplinary problems.

In order to begin developing transfer-level knowledge and skills, students should evaluate multiple contexts to derive learning intentions, success criteria, and transfer-level challenges.

This entire chapter is designated for this work, as it is essential for setting up the expectations for transfer. Given the work discussed in chapter 1 (page 17), students should be familiar with the purpose and practice of understanding and developing (that is, co-constructing) learning intentions and success criteria in surface-and-deep networks and as such will be well prepared for the application of such strategies as they transition to transfer learning. Teachers should follow these four steps to engage students in transfer-level work.

1. Develop transfer-level success criteria within and across disciplines.

2. Create multiple contexts for students to engage in surface and deep learning intentions and success criteria.

3. Construct transfer-level questions.

4. Co-develop transfer-level challenges and tasks.

Develop Transfer-Level Success Criteria Within and Across Disciplines

To engage students in transfer-level work, teachers need to establish transfer-level expectations by creating success criteria. Figure 2.1 (page 40) illustrates a number of sample transfer-level verbs that you may use to create transfer-level learning intentions and success criteria.

Transfer-Level Verbs
Students will design and conduct . . .
Students will formulate . . .
Students will generalize . . .
Students will hypothesize . . .
Students will initiate . . .
Students will reflect . . .
Students will research . . .

Figure 2.1: Rubric rhetoric.

When designing transfer-level learning intentions and success criteria, you may choose one of several approaches.

- ▸ Draft a single set of transfer criteria for one learning intention in an academic discipline.
- ▸ Combine multiple learning intentions in the same discipline.
- ▸ Combine multiple learning intentions across various disciplines.

Figure 2.2 provides a template you may use to design transfer-level learning intentions and success criteria. The appendices contain specific examples of transfer-level learning intentions and success criteria across all grade bands.

Let's look at an example of integrating surface and deep learning intentions and success criteria in English language arts and social studies. Figure 2.3 (page 42) illustrates concrete examples of surface- and deep-level learning intentions and success criteria in social studies. Figure 2.4 (page 42) shows surface- and deep-level learning intentions and success criteria in English language arts. Figure 2.5 (page 43) illustrates transfer-level success criteria for both learning intentions shown in figures 2.3 and 2.4. Note that there are numerous examples of developing transfer-level learning intentions in figure B.2 of appendix B (page 136).

Within Discipline, One Learning Intention	Within Discipline, Multiple Learning Intentions	Across Disciplines, Multiple Learning Intentions
Discipline A	**Discipline A**	**Discipline A**
Learning Intention		Learning Intention		Learning Intention	
Surface-Level Success Criteria		Surface-Level Success Criteria		Surface-Level Success Criteria	
Deep-Level Success Criteria		Deep-Level Success Criteria		Deep-Level Success Criteria	
		Discipline A		**Discipline B**	
Transfer-Level Success Criteria		Learning Intention		Learning Intention	
		Surface-Level Success Criteria		Surface-Level Success Criteria	
		Deep-Level Success Criteria		Deep-Level Success Criteria	
		Transfer-Level Success Criteria		Transfer-Level Success Criteria	

Figure 2.2: Transfer-level success-criteria template.

*Visit **go.SolutionTree.com/instruction** for a free reproducible version of this figure.*

Learning Intention	Students evaluate the cooperation and conflict that existed among the American Indians and between the Indian nations and the new settlers. (5.3)
Surface	• Describe the competition among the English, French, Spanish, Dutch, and Indian nations for control of North America. • Describe the cooperation that existed between the colonists and Indians during the 1600s and 1700s (for example, in agriculture, the fur trade, military alliances, treaties, and cultural interchanges). • Examine the conflicts before the Revolutionary War (for example, the Pequot and King Philip's Wars in New England, the Powhatan Wars in Virginia, and the French and Indian War). • Discuss the role of broken treaties and massacres and the factors that led to the Indians' defeat, including the resistance of Indian nations to encroachments and assimilation (for example, the Trail of Tears). • Describe the internecine Indian conflicts, including the competing claims for control of lands (for example, actions of the Iroquois, Huron, and Lakota). • Explain the influence and achievements of significant leaders of the time (for example, John Marshall, Andrew Jackson, Chief Tecumseh, Chief Logan, Chief John Ross, and Sequoyah).
Deep	• Compare and contrast cooperation and conflict between groups of people given our understanding of the cooperation and conflict that existed among the American Indians and between the Indian nations and the new settlers. • Analyze the cooperation and conflict between American Indians and between the Indian nations and the new settlers.

Source for standard: Adapted from California Department of Education, 2000.

Figure 2.3: Learning-intention and surface-and-deep success-criteria example, social studies.

Learning Intention	Write informative or explanatory texts to examine a topic and convey ideas and information clearly. (W.3.2)
Surface	• Introduce a topic and group related information together; include illustrations when useful to aiding comprehension. • Develop the topic with facts, definitions, and details. • Use linking words and phrases (for example, *also, another, and, more,* and *but*) to connect ideas within categories of information. • Provide a concluding statement or section.
Deep	• Relate the introduction of a topic to a concluding statement. • Relate the topic with facts, definitions, and details. • Apply the use of linking words to connect and contrast information within the writing.

Source for standard: Adapted from National Governors Association Center for Best Practices (NGA) & Council of Chief State School Officers (CCSSO), 2010a.

Figure 2.4: Learning-intention and surface-and-deep success-criteria example, English language arts.

Transfer	• Students write a hypothesis on how contemporary cooperation and conflict among groups within and across countries may be improved based on historical analysis.

Figure 2.5: Transfer success-criteria example.

Create Multiple Contexts for Students to Engage in Surface and Deep Learning Intentions and Success Criteria

Once teachers begin the process of designing transfer-level success criteria, the next step is to brainstorm different contexts that are relevant to the learning intentions. For example, many English language arts classes evaluate and explore the theme of power in books such as *1984* and *Fahrenheit 451*. These are typical *in-discipline* contexts. However, teachers can instruct students to consult other texts to extend their learning intentions to *out-of-discipline* contexts, such as gender and power dynamics in executive-leadership promotions and racial discrimination in gerrymandering.

In the case of the English language arts classroom, students can discuss the case of Israel Folau, who sued Rugby Australia for suspending him after he made remarks about specific groups of people on his social media page. This is an example of a context that teachers could use with students as a way for them to see how content applies in one or more situations. Students could then review the censorship guidelines of Facebook, Twitter, and other social media sites as they relate to banned media figures. These are typically out-of-discipline contexts. Table 2.1 illustrates several examples of in-discipline and out-of-discipline contexts.

Table 2.1: Examples of Developing Multiple Contexts

In-Discipline Contexts	Out-of-Discipline Contexts
Discipline: English language arts Students compare two texts that convey different themes (for example, *To Kill a Mockingbird* and *Lord of the Flies*).	Students listen to a number of podcasts and interview different people in their community to understand recurring themes of the human condition that are often conveyed in books.
Discipline: Statistics Students solve word problems using parametric statistics.	Students participate in a video conference with baseball analysts from a local college or a minor or major league baseball team to identify the important statistics they use to evaluate players.
Discipline: Chemistry Students conduct multiple lab experiments on diffusion.	Students visit researchers and explore a number of different case studies that are anchored in core standards (such as microbiology).

Construct Transfer-Level Questions

Teachers should set challenges for students through the creation of *driving questions*— questions that lead to transfer. This term refers to the momentum of a question to move students toward learning key background knowledge in order to solve a significant problem; the question drives the learning. These questions are designed to ensure students apply the surface and deep knowledge they have gained. Moreover, they should center on a common challenge within one context or across multiple contexts. Figure 2.6 shows a driving question with multiple contexts.

Contexts	Driving Question
• Rugby player Israel Folau • Facebook banning high-profile users • *1984* • *Fahrenheit 451*	To what extent should companies and governments censor speech?

Figure 2.6: Contexts and driving-question example.

Figure 2.7 offers several potential driving-question stems across transfer-level expectations. These stems are often associated with applying knowledge and skills.

Transfer-Level Verbs	Potential Driving-Question Stems
Design and Conduct	How would we . . . ?
Formulate	How would we . . . ?
Generalize	When would . . . ?
Hypothesize	Will . . . ?
Initiate	Should we . . . ?
Reflect	Who . . . ?
Research	To what extent . . . ?

Figure 2.7: Driving-question stems for transfer-level expectations.

As educational consultants Jay McTighe and Grant Wiggins (2013) suggest, the most important point in the development of driving questions is that "intent trumps form" (p. 7). That is, "*Why* you ask a question (in terms of the desired result of asking it) matters more than *how* you phrase it" (McTighe & Wiggins, 2013, p. 7). Here, we want to inspect the core point of the question we are asking. Because we spent significant time in chapter 1 (page 17) anchoring our work to the core standards of learning, we must now think about the relevance and impact the core standards have in the world. In essence, we want to work on problems that matter.

When creating driving questions, consider two factors: (1) the degree to which the challenge is purposeful to students and others and (2) the level of integration you expect within and across academic disciplines.

Common but weak driving questions might ask students how they would plan for and eliminate the threat of a zombie apocalypse, organize an exhibition on

Reconstruction as a museum curator, and recreate the double helix out of hobby-shop materials. The first question describes an impossible scenario, the second positions students to take on a professional role rather than apply their knowledge of the Reconstruction to a real-world problem, and the third simply reinforces surface-level knowledge. When designing challenging questions or situations, teachers should consider challenges that are realistic, require application, and affect students and the local and global community. Figure 2.8 offers a few examples of driving questions that are provocative and link to transfer-level expectations. Figure 2.9 illustrates a number of driving questions across disciplines and contexts.

- To what extent should preexisting symbols of prejudice be removed from the public square?
- Should entrance exams for advanced placement (AP) courses be removed from school policies?
- Should creationism be taught alongside evolution in science classes?
- How do we reconcile bullying in the second-grade classroom?

Figure 2.8: Driving-question examples.

Disciplines	Contexts	Driving Questions
• **Environmental studies** • **English language arts** • **Social studies**	• Shipping-lane speed limits • *Moby Dick*	• In what ways can we change the adversarial relationships that humans have with some animals? • To what extent should humans take responsibility for spaces such as oceans and outer space that are not owned by any species?
• **English language arts** • **Chemistry**	• *The Story of Glass* • *1984*	• To what extent can we ensure that the future prospects of all people are positively impacted by current and past technological innovations?
• **Biology** • **English language arts**	• *On the Origin of Species* • *Star Wars* • Social programs	• To what extent can humans control evolution in its many forms? • Should humans manipulate evolutionary processes?

Figure 2.9: Interdisciplinary driving questions.

The learning intentions and success criteria for each situation presented in figure 2.9 are available in figure B.2 of appendix B (page 136).

The process of creating transfer criteria, contexts, and challenges is iterative. Teachers often go back and forth between all aspects of transfer-level questions until they believe they have a clear line between each element. Figure 2.10 offers examples of all three aspects of contexts, transfer success criteria, and driving questions.

Potential Contexts	Transfer Success Criteria	Driving Questions
Building or refining the boundaries of a national park within proximity of human communities	Design and conduct a solution to real-life situations.	Should we manipulate the boundaries of a national park to alleviate human conflicts with animals?
Establishing a new endangered species in a common or contested space (for example, the ocean or disputed borders of a region or country)	Evaluate the implementation of a solution from one context to another context.	How do we protect animals that are in areas that are not owned by any nation?
Reintroducing a species	Critique a solution based on its alignment to core principles in a discipline, and describe any changes you would make to improve principle alignment.	To what extent should we reintroduce a species?
Removing an invasive species	Hypothesize the impact of different solutions to a problem in one or more contexts.	To what extent should we remove an invasive species?
Rescuing and treating indigenous flora and fauna	Apply elements of a solution from one context to a different context.	Should we save indigenous flora and fauna that are of no financial value to local communities?

Figure 2.10: Alignment of potential contexts, transfer success criteria, and driving questions.

Co-Develop Transfer-Level Challenges and Tasks

In chapter 1 (page 17), we looked at a co-development process in which students participated in determining the learning intentions and leveled success criteria. This process enabled students to understand the criteria for knowledge and skills required to identify and describe ideas and concepts (surface knowledge) and relate ideas and concepts (deep knowledge). Moreover, the process ensured students were prepared to give and receive effective feedback.

This chapter covers a similar process of student interaction with one another and their teachers; however, what students are searching for in this process is the actual relationship between different contexts. You must task students with finding an overarching driving question that links two contexts; from this process, students derive the criteria for transfer. As a result, students generate a list of surface and deep knowledge necessary to meet the expectations of the driving questions.

Suppose that a teacher presents students with two rate problems in mathematics, as shown in figure 2.11. One context involves two trains coming at each other from two different locations; the other context involves two boats traveling toward each other from two different locations.

Two trains leave different cities and head toward each other at different speeds. When and where do they meet?

Train A, traveling 70 miles per hour, leaves Westford heading toward Eastford, 260 miles away. At the same time, train B, traveling 60 miles per hour, leaves Eastford heading toward Westford. When do the two trains meet? How far from each city do they meet?

WESTFORD   **EASTFORD**

70 mph   **60 mph**

Two boats leave different cities and head toward each other at different speeds. When and where do they meet?

Sailboat A, traveling 4 knots (approximately 4.5 mph), leaves Sausalito heading toward San Francisco Giants Stadium, 12 miles away. At the same time, sailboat B, traveling 7 knots (approximately 8 mph), leaves San Francisco Giants Stadium heading toward Sausalito. When do the two boats meet? How far from each city do they meet?

Source: Adapted from Thomas, Brunsting, & Warrick, 2010.

Figure 2.11: Sample rate problems.

To engage in co-construction at transfer, teachers ask students to review both contexts (that is, trains and boats) and determine the related learning intentions and success criteria for each problem (see figure 2.12, page 48). A Venn diagram is the perfect tool for this. Teachers then instruct students to identify the overall driving question across both problems. Finally, students discuss the best way to demonstrate their transfer-level problem and solution. This problem could be showcased in a myriad of ways, including a presentation or a written explanation.

The rate problem in figure 2.11 presents a classic near-transfer problem, in which students must compare contexts and look at one specific learning intention in mathematics. The key to transfer for students is that they see how the operations of rate apply in different contexts. The solving of the actual rate problem lies within the surface-and-deep network. Figure 2.12 illustrates the success criteria for the rate problem.

Level of Complexity	Success Criteria
Surface	Use procedures to find distance, time, and relative rate (or relative speed).
Deep	Determine the relationship between distance, time, and rate. Since an equation remains true as long as we perform the same operation on both sides, we can divide both sides by rate: $$\frac{distance}{rate} = time$$ Or by time: $$\frac{distance}{time} = rate$$
Transfer	Apply operations in different contexts.

Figure 2.12: Leveled success criteria for rate.

Now, let's examine a more-complex problem that involves learning intentions and success criteria across multiple contexts and walk through the co-construction process with students. When designing near-to-far- and far-transfer-level work, individual teachers will need to incorporate learning intentions, success criteria, and contexts in different disciplines. Although collaborating with other teachers would be beneficial for engaging in designing transfer-level work for students, it isn't required practice.

Imagine that students must meet the learning intentions and success criteria shown in figure 2.13. As a means to move students toward transfer-level learning, a group of teachers take the following actions.

▸ Create transfer-level success criteria that relate to the underlying surface and deep knowledge in each content area.

▸ Identify a set of transfer-level driving questions.

▸ Develop several contextual problems that students must evaluate to understand the underlying surface and deep knowledge and to solve a problem, or problems, to meet transfer-level success criteria.

After considering the learning intentions and success criteria in figure 2.13, a group of teachers decides on this transfer success criterion: *propose solutions for countries to prevent or limit imperialism and enhance local assets.*

The teachers select and present two contexts for students: (1) antipoaching efforts in Mozambique and (2) marine-mammal rescue and rehabilitation in Marin County.

Teachers inform students about a large uptick in elephant poaching in the Maputo Special Reserve, near the capital of Mozambique. They then ask students, "To what extent should the government of Mozambique ensure the protection of an important

Content Area	Learning Intention	Surface	Deep
Biology	• I will use mathematical or computational representations to support explanations of factors that affect the carrying capacity of ecosystems at different scales. (HS-LS2–1)	• Define *carrying capacity*, *ecosystem*, *living* and *nonliving resources*, and *environment*. • Define *predation*, *competition*, and *disease*. • Identify mathematical or computational representations that are used in analyzing populations.	• Relate the relationships between environments and resources to population growth. • Compare and contrast living and nonliving resources to an ecosystem's carrying capacity. • Relate predation, competition, and disease to organism survival. • Relate computational representations to population change in one situation.
Statistics	• I will make inferences and justify conclusions from sample surveys, experiments, and observational studies. (HSS.IC.B)	• Recognize the purposes of and differences among sample surveys, experiments, and observational studies; explain how randomization relates to each. (HSS.IC.B.3)	• Use data from a sample survey to estimate a population mean or proportion; develop a margin of error through the use of simulation models for random sampling. (HSS.IC.B.4) • Use data from a randomized experiment to compare two treatments; use simulations to decide whether differences between parameters are significant. (HSS.IC.B.5) • Evaluate reports based on data. (HSS.IC.B.6)
English Language Arts	• I will write arguments to support claims in an analysis of substantive topics or texts, using valid reasoning and relevant and sufficient evidence. (W.9–10.1)	• Introduce precise, knowledgeable claims; establish the significance of the claims; distinguish the claims from alternate or opposing claims; and create an organization that logically sequences claims, counterclaims, reasons, and evidence. (W.9–10.1.A)	• Use words, phrases, and clauses, as well as varied syntax, to link the major sections of the text, create cohesion, and clarify the relationships between claims and reasons, between reasons and evidence, and between claims and counterclaims. (W.9–10.1.C)

Figure 2.13: Leveled success criteria across curriculum standards.

continued →

Content Area	Learning Intention	Surface	Deep
English Language Arts		• Develop claims and counter-claims fairly and thoroughly, supplying the most relevant evidence for each while pointing out the strengths and limitations of both in a manner that anticipates the audience's knowledge level, concerns, values, and possible biases. (W.9–10.1.B) • Establish and maintain a formal style and objective tone while attending to the norms and conventions of the discipline. (W.9–10.1.D) • Provide a concluding statement or section that follows from and supports the argument presented. (W.9–10.1.E)	
Social Studies	• I will analyze patterns of global change in the era of New Imperialism in at least two of the following regions or countries: Africa, Southeast Asia, China, India, Latin America, and the Philippines. (10.4)	• Describe the rise of industrial economies (for example, the role played by national security and strategic advantage; moral issues raised by the search for national hegemony, social Darwinism, and the missionary impulse; and material issues such as land, resources, and technology). (10.4.1) • Discuss the locations of the colonial rule of such nations as England, France, Germany, Italy, Japan, the Netherlands, Russia, Spain, Portugal, and the United States. (10.4.2) • Explain imperialism from the perspective of the colonizer and the colonized and the varied immediate and long-term responses by the people under colonial rule. (10.4.3) • Describe the independence struggles of the colonized regions of the world, including the roles of leaders, such as Sun Yat-sen in China, and the roles of ideology and religion. (10.4.4)	• Link imperialism and colonialism of industrial economies. • Discuss the implications of the location of the colonizers and the colonized. • Evaluate the perspectives of colonizers and the colonized. • Analyze the behavior of colonizers and the colonized given the perspectives of both groups.

Source for standards: Adapted from California Department of Education, 2000; NGA & CCSSO, 2010b; NGSS Lead States, 2013.

resource for international tourism and general national interests while balancing the economic disparities in and around Maputo?"

Next, the teachers present students with a list of seals, sea lions, and sea otters that have been rescued and are currently being rehabilitated at the Marine Mammal Center in Sausalito, California. Through a brief review, students determine that most of the animals faced direct and indirect interactions with humans. Teachers ask students, "Who is responsible for managing marine mammals?"

From here, students evaluate the similarities and differences between both contexts—in this case, Mozambique tourism and local economics, and North Pacific marine-mammal rescue. Figure 2.14 illustrates the responses students might produce.

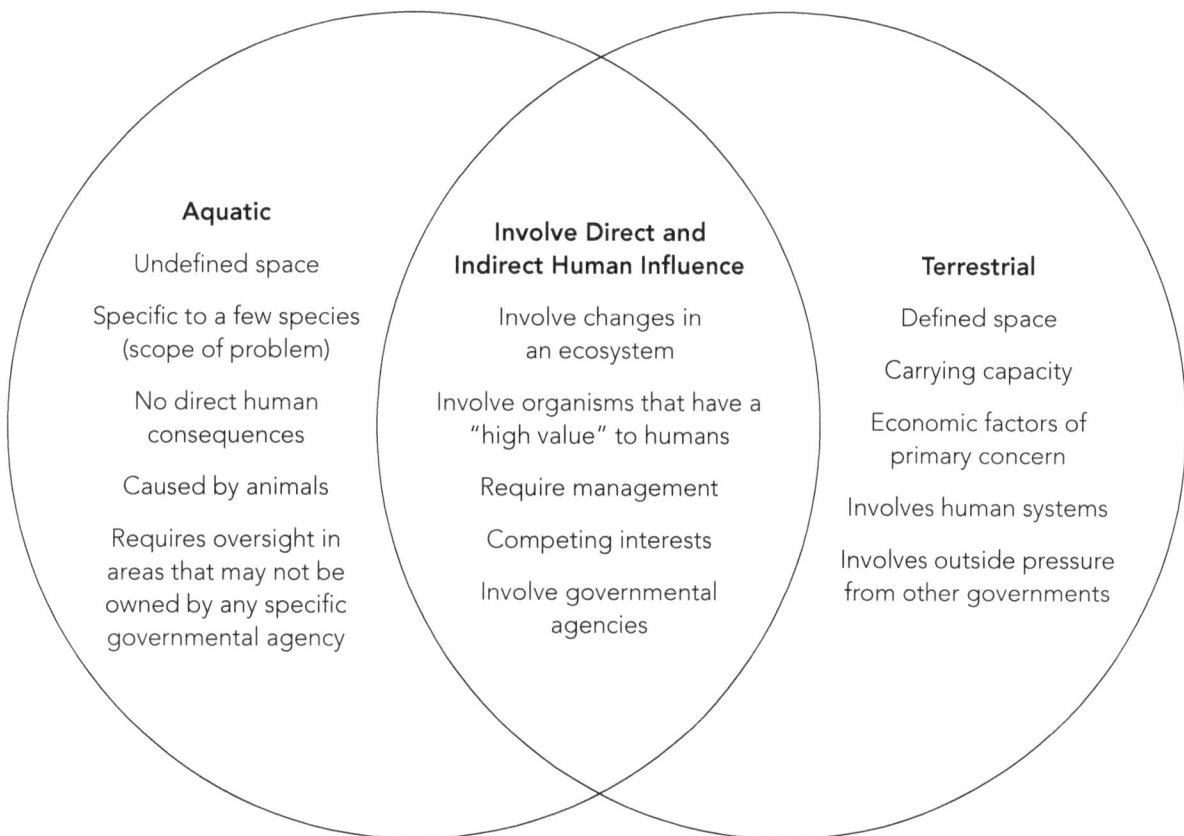

Aquatic

Undefined space

Specific to a few species (scope of problem)

No direct human consequences

Caused by animals

Requires oversight in areas that may not be owned by any specific governmental agency

Involve Direct and Indirect Human Influence

Involve changes in an ecosystem

Involve organisms that have a "high value" to humans

Require management

Competing interests

Involve governmental agencies

Terrestrial

Defined space

Carrying capacity

Economic factors of primary concern

Involves human systems

Involves outside pressure from other governments

Figure 2.14: Venn diagram example.

Once students have evaluated both contexts, teachers task them with creating a driving question (or driving questions) that connects both contexts—for example, To what extent should societies limit economic and social activities that impact local and global ecosystems? Next, the teachers go back and share the surface- and deep-level learning intentions and success criteria that students need to learn to successfully answer the driving question. Finally, teachers ask students to identify ways they could represent their solutions to others. In this approach, students have significant autonomy in demonstrating their surface and deep knowledge and presenting their answers to the driving question: presentations, written explanations, podcasts, and the like.

Conclusion

When students face more than one context, they have an opportunity to transfer surface and deep knowledge to a problem. The degree of difficulty is dependent on how many contexts and disciplines you present to students. Ultimately, student participation in determining the core problem is key to their engaging in transfer-level learning and investing in, or reinforcing, surface and deep knowledge. The activities in this chapter provided a template and several examples of designing for transfer.

Reflection Questions

The following questions are designed for you to address individually or in teams to determine the next steps that you will take in the classroom. When you review these questions, it is important that you reflect on the tools you currently use with students and where you may discover tension between your current beliefs and practices and what I've proposed. Educators usually carry with them a set of tools that work well in certain situations. This chapter's contents may have been somewhat familiar to those teachers who have tools that work well in the garage. Teachers who come with a set of tools suited to the office, however, may have found this chapter challenging. Regardless of where you stand, this is an opportunity for you to incorporate new tools.

1. What was surprising in this chapter? What do you know now that you didn't know prior to reading this chapter?

2. How are transfer design steps similar to or different from those of your current design?

3. What is most doable and practical for you to engage in with students?

Next Steps

As with the reflection questions, please go through each of these steps individually or as a team and determine what actions you will take in your classroom.

1. With a small teacher group, ask each person to record answers to the following series of questions.

   a. What is one key takeaway from this reading?

   b. What is one tension that you faced when reading this chapter? What challenges your current beliefs or practices?

   c. What is something you want to try tomorrow?

   Next, have teachers discuss their responses with the group. Ultimately, the answers may be used to identify individual and team goals.

2. Please review the examples of units at near transfer, near-to-far transfer, and far transfer in appendix B (figures B.3, B.4, and B.5, respectively, pages 140–144). Visit **go.SolutionTree.com/instruction** to download these templates, and then create your own units for near transfer, near-to-far transfer, and far transfer.

3. Once you have created these units, go through a critical-friends protocol with other faculty (see figure A.5 in appendix A, page 132). In the next few chapters, we will be adding to these units.

4. Role-play with faculty or a sample group of students on the co-construction of the driving question. After role-playing, conduct a feedback process (for example, the learning-dilemma protocol in figure A.6 of appendix A, page 133) on the co-construction process.

5. Create questions for surface-, deep-, and transfer-level expectations of a unit. One way to do this is to think of success criteria as answers to questions at each level of complexity; see figure 2.15. Figure 2.16 (page 54) provides examples for teachers to review before creating their own questions.

Surface	Deep	Transfer
Who . . . ? What . . . ? How . . . ?	Why . . . ?	Should . . . ? When . . . ? Where . . . ? To what extent . . . ?

Figure 2.15: Leveled question stems.

Content Area	Surface	Deep	Near Transfer	Far Transfer
Civics and Government	• How do we provide checks and balances on governmental power?	• Why do we provide checks and balances on governmental power?	• In what ways does the Constitution attempt to limit abuse of governmental powers? • Where do the Constitution's attempts to limit abuse of governmental powers fail to meet 21st century issues? • Should the government have a say in what people do?	• Where should limits be set with regard to special education rights and individuals' and educational institutions' responsibilities?
Literature	• What makes a great story? • How do effective writers hook and hold their readers?	• Why do stories attempt to hook readers' attention in different ways? • Why do great stories follow recurring patterns?	• To what extent can others create unique hooks in stories that follow a common pattern? • Should stories continue to follow recurring patterns? • To what extent can stories illuminate the human condition?	• Should we use storytelling to enable others to understand complex topics?
Visual Arts	• What formal qualities of art are conveyed in this piece? • How does art convey recurring themes?	• Why do humans convey the human condition in works of art?	• Who has been impacted by these works of art?	• Where can we influence future generations in making better decisions?
Science	• What are key biomolecules that make up our diet? • How does my diet affect my life?	• Why do particular biomolecules positively and negatively influence our diet?	• Whom can we believe about dietary matters?	• To what extent is truth a stable entity?

Mathematics	• What is addition? • How do we add?	• Why does adding two like quantities in different ways always provide the same sum?	• To what extent is addition limiting to our ability to understand the world?	• To what extent should addition be the method used for situations that require multiple numbers and occasional reductions?
Physical Education	• What are effective offensive and defensive strategies in individual and team games? • How do we use offensive and defensive strategies?	• What is the key relationship between offensive and defensive strategies?	• Where do cooperation and competition simultaneously occur in games?	• When should competitive strategies be used versus cooperative strategies?

Source: Adapted from McTighe & Wiggins, 2013.

Figure 2.16: Surface, deep, and transfer questions.

Chapter 3

Introducing Change in the Learning Experience:
Leveraging Perspective and Perplexity

*I brought home outdated racist insults from school like it was the
1950s. All Mexican slurs, of course, since people where I grew up
don't know Natives still exist. That's how much those Oakland
hills separate us from Oakland. Those hills bend time.*

—TOMMY ORANGE

Transfer learning requires a fundamental change in the mind of a learner both cognitively and affectively. For instance, in many cases, transfer learning requires people to understand the perspectives of others. How we see the world, other people, and ourselves differently and respond based on new ideas, or old ideas viewed differently, is a major part of transfer learning. Beyond this, exploring other angles to a problem, considering alternative ways of representing knowledge, and finding similarities across multiple situations are part and parcel of transfer.

But we must also take into account the inevitable changes that people face as they are working on problems. Often when people engage in real-world problems, things break, materials for a solution are unavailable, or variables outside their control complicate the problem. From changes in the market to natural disasters and human-induced catastrophes, people inevitably must face changes that emerge. Transfer learning, then, requires a learner to deftly negotiate those unexpected occurrences.

Transfer is fundamentally built on change, and this chapter focuses on your introducing to the student experience the kind of change and fluidity that is not typically part of surface-and-deep-network development. Providing opportunities for students to view the world through a prism of perspectives and address problems and situations that constantly shift because of known and unknown forces is essential for supporting students in developing transfer learning.

These student experiences yield an impact that moves beyond the classroom—an authenticity of the world beyond one's own perspective and a realism of the changes that people actually face in society, social situations, and work life. To heighten relevance to students and make adaptation to change a more significant aspect of students' learning experiences, teachers must *create perspective* and *craft perplexity*. Creating perspective, or new ways of looking at a subject, involves designing collisions of ideas and beliefs as part of instructional practice. Crafting perplexity is a teaching technique in which students learn how to overcome changes within and across tasks and contexts. Changing a student's vantage point or expectations of a task, or making adjustments in or across contexts in the middle of a unit of instruction, is uncomfortable for both students and teachers. However, it is the actual nature of transfer-level work and perhaps the truest sense of authenticity we can apply in our classrooms.

Figure 3.1 illustrates the success criteria for both students and teachers in creating perspective and crafting perplexity. This chapter offers a blueprint for incorporating this level of change in the classroom.

Change in the Learning Experience	Students encounter changes in:	Effective teaching strategies include:
Students face varied dynamics through the learning process to enhance transfer learning and mimic real-world challenges.	☐ Others' perspectives within and across contexts ☐ Task structure or task expectations ☐ Success criteria ☐ Contexts	☐ Introducing a variety of perspectives within the transfer challenge ☐ Switching the task structure or augmenting task expectations during a unit of study ☐ Adjusting success criteria to include more nuanced or complex expectations for students ☐ Bringing in different tools and rules within the success criteria ☐ Incorporating new contexts, or new information within an existing context, before, during, or after the unit of study

Figure 3.1: Change-in-the-learning-experience success criteria.

*Visit **go.SolutionTree.com/instruction** for a free reproducible version of this figure.*

Preparing for Change

Perspective and perplexity are two key elements of change for students. As such, students will need to know the steps required to handle stress, setbacks, and situations that challenge their beliefs, behaviors, and backgrounds. As discussed in chapter 1 (page 17), the efficacy-based approaches of orientation, activation, and collaboration are immensely helpful for students to navigate the changes they will inherently face when engaging in transfer-level work. Students need to leverage the activation-based strategies of *focusing forward* and *then and now* (page 34) to effectively handle perplexity- and perspective-based situations. This base-level familiarity with activation will eventually lead to mastery of the skill of activation, which chapter 4 (page 73) outlines as a key element of moving transfer learning forward for students.

Creating Perspective

To deepen surface- and deep-level knowledge and apply it to different situations, students need to encounter a multitude of viewpoints related to learning intentions, success criteria, and contexts. In mathematics, students need to see visual representations of algorithms; in English language arts, they need to explore the motivations of antagonists; and in history, they need to explore perspectives of groups of people who have largely been marginalized or omitted from the common narrative of the discipline. For example, in this chapter's epigraph, author Tommy Orange writes about how certain people in the Bay Area have failed to evaluate established beliefs about and behaviors toward other races and as such have perpetuated a set of biases and prejudices that has stood the test of time. Our job as teachers is to challenge such accepted "truths" by, as scholar Stephen Brookfield (1986) argues, "analyzing assumptions, challenging previously accepted and internalized beliefs and values, [and] considering the validity of alternative behaviors" (p. 125).

In order to enhance student perspective, I propose the following teacher actions.

▸ Refine driving questions to evoke multiple perspectives.

▸ Employ reading, writing, and talking tasks that ensure all voices are heard.

▸ Use specific protocols that ensure all voices are heard.

Refine Driving Questions to Evoke Multiple Perspectives

Suppose you were faced with the question, Who defines heroism in the 21st century?

How would you go about approaching this question? Would you start from your own experience of defining heroism? Would you look to those individuals and groups who have authority in the government or media? Would you look to the voices of those from marginalized groups?

In one class, a teacher might use this question to explore divergent perspectives, starting out by having students read two texts on Christopher Columbus's arrival to the Americas—one from the perspective of the explorer and the other from the perspective of the natives who encountered the explorer. The teacher might ask students, "Is an explorer a hero to those who live in the area being explored?" This leads to a powerful conversation on the need for multiple perspectives when answering the driving question, Who defines heroism in the 21st century?

Let's look at a personal example. In the summer of 2017, a Harvard graduate and colleague of mine stated that Juul, the electronic cigarette company, was on a hiring spree at Harvard Business School. The number of job solicitations in the area of marketing and advertising for the company was impressive, or scary. Coincidentally, the following year, I read an article titled "The Promise of Vaping and the Rise of Juul" by Jia Tolentino (2018). In the article, Tolentino makes the argument that through effective marketing, children have embraced this new technology of smoking and see it as displacing Big Tobacco. They also don't view this nicotine-laden technology as addictive! Imagine a driving question such as, Should we engage in activities that provide a net benefit economically for employees and businesses even when they negatively impact society? Beyond Juul, we could look at the evaluation of our national and local governments as they weigh citizens' safety and the economic costs related to the COVID-19 pandemic.

Let's look at a few more examples: Straws are a terrible health hazard to marine animals, but they are incredibly handy when people want to drink orange juice. *To what extent should local governments provide oversight over straw usage?* Mathematics is often expressed in standard algorithmic form in schools, but using arrays, graphs, number lines, charts, and qualification data enables others to see numbers in different ways. *Where can we best leverage the diversity of interpretations of mathematics in our work?*

Figure 3.2 provides suggested success criteria for perspective-laden driving questions.

Employ Reading, Writing, and Talking Tasks That Ensure All Voices Are Heard

One way to ensure students develop both surface-and-deep networks and transfer networks is to have students engage in tasks that are anchored in reading, writing, and talking. Moreover, these tasks should include multiple perspectives. For example, if a history teacher wants students to explore the Iran-Contra Affair through a reading activity, the teacher should bring in texts that offer a range of accounts from Central America and the Middle East to illustrate perspectives that differ from the U.S. viewpoint.

Suggested Criteria	Description	Examples
Driving questions that evoke multiple perspectives	Driving questions that evoke multiple perspectives require students to listen to voices that are not commonly heard in major texts, film, and other media. This may involve seeking the perspectives of those from the LGBTQ+ community, Native Americans, African Americans, people with disabilities, women, and other groups.	• Who defines heroism? • Who makes the rules? • To what extent does the Black Lives Matter movement influence local governance in conservative communities and new approaches to evaluating history and generating different types of literature? • To what extent can communities address bias and moral licensing? • Should the wealthy pay more taxes for others to gain benefits and have better opportunities to compete against them? • Where should the economically or racially privileged have their power limited in making decisions that ultimately benefit their traditional financial and social power?
Driving questions that ensure multiple answers, or multiple explanations of an answer	Driving questions that evoke multiple answers or approaches give people the opportunity to recognize and appreciate the complexity of authentic real-life problems.	• Should we change the way in which presidents are elected? • Who should ultimately be responsible for gun violence? • Where does mathematics influence our perspective on ideas we care about?

Figure 3.2: Perspective-laden driving-question criteria.

Another reading task might require students to examine the way statistics are conveyed to an audience. By showing students how numbers communicated differently can influence and manipulate our perspectives, students will have a better sense of the power of mathematics across contexts. Through evaluating car and home loan options, using statistics to assess baseball players' performance, and determining the best options for investing in various kinds of energy, they'll see how different people and organizations emphasize certain statistics and simply downplay or ignore other essential information.

Similar claims could be made regarding the choices Americans make when selecting news to read and watch; from MSNBC to Fox News, to Reddit and Facebook feeds, people are continually seeking out information that reaffirms their beliefs and opinions. As Wexler (2019) states, "When new information is inconsistent with our existing beliefs, we experience mental discomfort—which we resolve by rejecting the information, regardless of the evidence. Psychologists call this tendency *confirmation bias*" (p. 75). In *The Intelligence Trap*, science journalist David Robson (2019) refers to confirmation bias as *myside bias* and writes that more intelligent people—those who possess a strong set of surface and deep knowledge and skills—are no more likely than anyone else to consider alternative points of view.

Regardless of the specific lesson, teachers can incorporate both talking and writing tasks to highlight these alternative points of view. For example, before initiating a discussion about the Iran-Contra Affair, a teacher may ask each student to engage in a think-pair-share activity with another student. The teacher instructs students to write down their initial beliefs and understandings regarding the cause of the conflict. Next, students pair up with new partners, sharing out their responses. The teacher may repeat this exercise during and after the unit of study. This enables the students to reflect on their key learning over time and the value of evaluating different perspectives.

Providing students with opportunities to scan a range of opinions, find common interests, look closely at shared and disparate values, and consider different approaches to problems gives students a better sense of other people and the ways others interpret and act on the world. This enables students to more effectively solve problems with and for others.

Figure 3.3 shows reading, writing, and talking tasks that infuse multiple perspectives.

Task Type	Core Tasks	Questions on Missing Voices to Leverage
Reading	Surface: Preview a passage and highlight key ideas. Reflect on other passages that convey a different set of key ideas. Deep: Annotate where key implications about relationships and principles become apparent. Transfer: Find other texts that draw on similar implications and principles from a different context.	Does this text represent the groups of people who were impacted during this time period, this issue, or this innovation? How can we bring in additional perspectives?
Writing	Surface: List and describe key ideas. Deep: Construct a thesis statement that depicts the relationships between key ideas. Transfer: Write an opinion piece.	To what extent does our writing represent and respect others' perspectives?
Talking	Surface: Recite key ideas. Deep: Argue for or against the key principles presented in a passage. Transfer: Analyze how the key principles and implications from the assigned passage relate to a new context in front of a panel.	Do our language, rhetoric, and approach to persuading others indicate an appreciation of others? What biases are we bringing to this discussion?

Figure 3.3: Perspective-laden reading, writing, and talking tasks.

Use Specific Protocols That Ensure All Voices Are Heard

A core part of emphasizing perspective is to ensure that classroom discussions include all *students'* voices. One way to do so is to use protocols that enable groups to structure conversations when discussing and making decisions. The correct protocol can also heighten the effectiveness of feedback and make students feel safe and respected. Table 3.1 shares a number of protocols that ensure multiple perspectives are represented in discussions and decision making.

Table 3.1: Perspective-Laden Protocols

Protocol	Description	Activity
Challenging Assumptions	Students generate a set of assumptions that may be influencing their own beliefs and actions, as well as those of the people they are learning about.	Students: • Identify the key decisions or implications of a situation • Identify who is impacted by a decision • Brainstorm key assumptions that were used to make a decision and the implications of the decision • Analyze the level of success of a decision given the assumptions generated • Develop potential solutions that would have offered better approaches to all parties involved or impacted by the decision within the context of the situation
Flipping Perspective	Students engage in exploring the perspectives of groups who are impacted by decisions and have varied racial, political, social, or economic standings in order to advocate for a different solution.	Students: • Identify the key decisions or implications of a situation • Craft perspectives from different stakeholders, looking through the lens of race, politics, society, and economics • Brainstorm potential next steps to create a successful solution
Plus Sum	Students generate a set of solutions that have the best chance of positively influencing beliefs, attitudes, and decision making for all parties involved.	Students: • Identify the key decisions or implications of a situation • Identify who is impacted by a decision • Brainstorm key assumptions that were used to make a decision and the implications of the decision • Create potential solutions that fall into one of four categories: (1) improvements, (2) shortfall, (3) opportunities, or (4) new venture • Focus on potential solutions that enhance the lives of all stakeholders • Generate short-term and long-term implications of their proposed solution

Crafting Perplexity

Though journalist Anderson Cooper was well established in 2004, he found him-self in a precarious position reporting in Haiti—one in which he was left without the resources he had grown accustomed to and would need to cover a coup d'état. The military personnel with whom he was traveling by bus told Cooper and other reporters to exit the vehicle and leave the premises of the city.

Cooper got off the bus and found his gear sitting in a puddle of sewage. As the story goes, he remained at the bus while other news anchors hopped in SUVs and traveled to safe locations to rest. Having nowhere to go, Cooper (2018) headed into the danger zone and found a nearby hospital, where he interviewed citizens and learned about the impact of the coup.

Cooper was constrained by a lack of access to resources that would have allowed him safe harbor from danger. Moreover, as conditions changed, he had to adapt, constantly seeking new stories and new angles to stories that were previously unavail-able. He tapped into the ingenuity he'd developed at the very start of his career, when he'd been forced to make fake press passes to get to places like Burma with just a backpack and his camera, sleeping on roofs and hitching rides—likely getting him closer to the action than seasoned reporters at the time (Cooper, 2018). Emerging constraints and constant changes in situations are powerful motivators, as they require us to think through—and think differently about—how to solve problems.

Students need to grapple with this kind of perplexity in their daily routine. Perplexity is all about working through situations that are baffling and uncomfort-able, and there are many ways for students to encounter it in the classroom—through new challenges that emerge in a problem, new tasks, new contexts, and so forth.

The following two strategies are designed to enable students to handle perplexity.

1. Change the task.

2. Incorporate new contexts before, during, or after the unit.

Change the Task

Picture a scenario in which students are midway through completing an essay assignment and the teacher announces that they now must conduct a two-minute oral synopsis of what they are writing. Or suppose the scenario is flipped and stu-dents have to draft an executive summary of an oral presentation.

Let's dream up another situation. Suppose a student is learning about microbiol-ogy and immunology and working through a case study in physiology. Her job is to diagnose a patient with a particular ailment and create a treatment plan evaluating the efficacy of the prognosis. Over the course of a few weeks, she reviews blood sam-ples, finds that the patient has a bacterial infection, and identifies the best antibiotics to treat the patient. However, the day before the presentation, the student receives a notice that the information she received was incorrect and that the lab results illustrating microorganisms in the blood were wrong. She now must go back to the drawing board with only a day to spare.

Imagine another situation, in which a student is creating a narrative and the success criteria require him to end with a concluding statement. However, the teacher announces that new success criteria have been "unlocked," or "opened," and now the student must end with a metaphor or a cliff-hanger. Perhaps, on the same day, the student enters his physics class and is told that he is unable to ignore air resistance in the unit he's working on. He then goes to economics, where, in a unit on investing, he finds out that he must navigate a housing-market change in a transfer task because the Federal Reserve increased interest rates. Then, in mathematics, he must illustrate his mathematics in multiple ways to convey an understanding to numerous stakeholder groups—ranging from nonproficient laypeople to expert mathematicians. Clearly this is a tough day for this particular student!

These back-to-back curveballs may sound unlikely in an academic setting, but they mirror those setbacks, big and small, that people encounter in everyday life. Even more interesting is that they force people to step back and make sure that their surface-and-deep networks are intact. Students must focus on what matters in the academic discipline and not just be geared toward completing a task. Additionally, these changes provide students a better opportunity to transfer, as they must home in on the outcomes within and between problems and contexts. Figure 3.4 offers a number of ways for teachers to create changes in student actions and activities.

Changing the Task	Example
Rearrange reading, writing, and talking tasks.	Ask students to shift from an oral presentation to a written document (or vice versa).
Introduce a variable in the problem.	Have students abandon their study of a bacterial infection and instead examine a fungal, protist, or viral infection.
Open up success criteria.	Instruct students to replace a concluding statement with a metaphor or a cliff-hanger.
Adjust tools and rules.	Require students to incorporate visual displays and multiple representations of their mathematics work.

Figure 3.4: Approaches to changing the task.

Incorporate New Contexts Before, During, or After the Unit

In chapter 2 (page 37), we looked at a transfer-level problem that asked students to analyze two contexts. The first was about elephant poaching, and the second was about marine-mammal rescue and rehabilitation. Imagine if, at the end of the transfer-level unit, teachers ask students to analyze a new context, such as addressing the challenges resulting from the ferret's introduction into New Zealand. Ferrets were introduced in the late 1800s to eliminate rabbits on farmland. However, this invasive species has also caused the rapid decline of the many flightless birds in New Zealand, including the kakapo and the kiwi. Teachers may have students re-evaluate the solutions they proposed for elephant poaching and marine-mammal rescue and rehabilitation, and determine whether their solutions apply in this new context. Students would also evaluate what surface- and deep-level knowledge is critical when evaluating this context. Finally, to account for students' need to consider other perspectives, teachers may instruct students to evaluate the view of government officials, farmers, conservationists, and the Maori people of New Zealand. The sky is the limit.

Contextual changes could happen during a unit of study as well. Imagine a teacher is instructing students about how laws are created and implemented. Here, the teacher is interested in providing her students with a multitude of perspectives to understand the impact of laws on humankind and the influence certain groups of people have on the development of laws. Suppose she begins by teaching students core content on federal civil rights and voting rights. Next, she places students into four groups and has each group explore a different set of articles, videos, and textbook passages on the implementation or absence of laws in communities.

Following this initial review, students form new groups, sharing similarities and differences between the various contexts and formulating questions that develop from the intersection of all contexts. Student groups then present their questions, and together, the class selects a driving question for the remainder of the unit.

In multiple transfer situations, there are numerous contexts that can be compared and contrasted, as represented by the Venn diagram in figure 3.5.

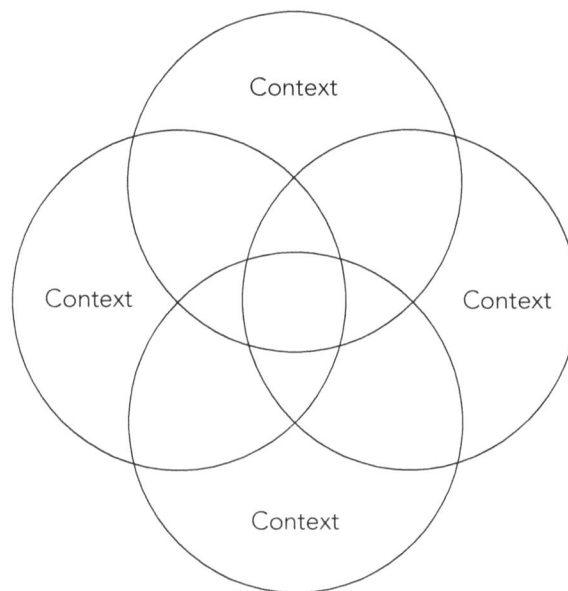

Figure 3.5: Visual representation of multiple transfer situations.

Or, perhaps at the beginning of a unit of study, a teacher gives students unique case files of patients who recently arrived at a local hospital. The case files contain descriptions of the patients' conditions—information on symptoms and early testing results but no diagnosis or prognosis—that the students must investigate. The teacher then instructs students to identify what they need to know in the areas of microbiology and immunology to assist doctors in treating the patients. As students work to tackle their cases, the teacher may add elements of perplexity, providing new developments from the hospital that require students to change their diagnoses and prognoses or swapping students' case files. Throughout this work, students must constantly seek additional surface- and deep-level knowledge to apply to their cases.

Figure 3.6 illustrates three different activities teachers may engage in with students to apply core content across a multitude of contexts. Indeed, there are countless ways for teachers to bring in new scenarios and change contexts within a unit of learning.

Contextual Activity	Description	Example
From Franchise to Sequel	After students initially look at one context, teachers give them a brand-new context to analyze and compare to other contexts.	Students: • Solve a problem within a context (for example, write a persuasive essay on whether students should wear school uniforms) • Receive a new problem (for example, write a persuasive essay on whether students should be able to pick their own teachers) • Reflect on the similarities and differences between both contexts and the content they are learning
Choose Your Own Adventure	Teachers give students multiple contexts to select and analyze while they learn surface and deep knowledge. During the unit of instruction, students compare and contrast different scenarios and case studies with other students.	Students: • Receive a case study (for example, a patient with a particular disease) • Discuss their case study with other students to determine the similarities and differences between the context and the content
World Café	Teachers give individual students a multitude of scenarios and ask that they share, in groups, similarities and differences between the scenarios. Visit the World Café Community Foundation (2015; www.theworldcafe.com) for more information on this method. (Visit **go.SolutionTree .com/instruction** to access direct links to the resources mentioned in this book.)	Students: • Receive one or more contexts to analyze (for example, water contamination and waste exportation) • Determine the key success criteria that they use to analyze the context (content-based criteria) • Engage in a world-café protocol to share their problem or solution with others

Figure 3.6: Context-based activities.

Conclusion

Where surface-and-deep networks are all about smooth sailing, transfer networks are about navigating rough waters. Perspective is one of the key elements of change students face as they begin to look at the scope of a situation, topic, or problem. Encountering questions that require multiple perspectives; completing tasks that intentionally focus their minds on reading, writing, and talking about the viewpoints of others; and utilizing structured ways to discuss diverse opinions all enable students to apply a breadth and depth of knowledge to situations.

Moreover, transfer networks require that students encounter perplexity as a component of problem solving. The primary driver of perplexity for students is the variable of change—change in contexts, task expectations, and success criteria. As such, students will need a set of skills to apply their learning, handle change on an individual level, and engage with others. Chapters 4 (page 73) and 5 (page 97) lay out how teachers can prepare students to do just that.

Reflection Questions

The following questions are designed for you to address individually or in teams to determine the next steps that you will take in the classroom. When you review these questions, it is important that you reflect on the tools you currently use with students and where you may discover tension between your current beliefs and practices and what I've proposed. Educators usually carry with them a set of tools that work well in certain situations. This chapter's contents may have been somewhat familiar to those teachers who have tools that work well in the garage. Teachers who come with a set of tools suited to the office, however, may have found this chapter challenging. Regardless of where you stand, this is an opportunity for you to incorporate new tools.

1. How do you currently introduce different perspectives into your unit design and implementation?

2. How do you currently introduce perplexity into your unit design and implementation?

3. How do you ensure that students are engaging in the elements of perspective and perplexity?

4. What stood out for you in this chapter?

5. What skills do you foresee students needing as they encounter change in learning?

Next Steps

As with the reflection questions, please go through each of these steps individually or as a team and determine what actions you will take in your classroom.

1. Engage in one of the activities in figure 3.7 with students in the classroom, and then debrief with both colleagues and students on the key takeaways regarding perspective and perplexity.

Activity	Description
Perspective: Got global?	Ask students to find local and global views on a specific idea, issue, or person. Next, ask students to identify potential reasons for shared and divergent views. Finally, ask students what next steps should be taken to develop a shared understanding of differences and ways to develop collective approaches to local and global problems.
Perplexity: Create the next great sequel!	Ask students to draw up a new context to investigate the learning intention and success criteria. Next, have students build in potential challenges that people would realistically face if engaging in that problem in that context. Finally, have students walk through their thinking processes.
Perplexity: So then that happened!	After giving students a challenge, ask them to reflect on the following prompts. • What challenges are you facing? • What changes are you going to need to make? • How are you going to begin this process? • How do you feel right now? • What next steps will you take to stay emotionally calm when facing challenges?
Perplexity: Choose your own adventure.	Provide students with a multitude of scenarios or case studies, and allow them to choose one to investigate or study.

Figure 3.7: Perspective- and perplexity-based activities.

2. After crafting the transfer units (near, near-to-far, and far) in chapter 2 (page 37), consider adding elements of perspective and perplexity.

3. Go back and review the next steps in chapter 2 (page 37), and determine whether you are going to make any changes.

4. Exchange feedback with colleagues on a number of units with the additional elements of perspective and perplexity; use, for example, the critical-friends protocol (page 132).

5. Conduct a pre- and postlesson focus group with a cohort of students on how their perspectives changed after engaging in a unit of

study involving multiple perspectives. Suggested questions include the following.

    a. On a scale of 1–5 (5 being the most valuable), what value do you place on perspectives other than those from your textbook, your teacher, and yourself?

    b. How do you currently seek out other perspectives?

    c. What does it mean to you when you hear, read, or see a perspective that is different from your own?

    d. What strategies do you use to ensure you listen to others when they share information you have never heard before or opinions you disagree with?

6. Conduct a pre- and postlesson focus group with a cohort of students on how they view and handle perplexity after engaging in a unit of study involving multiple perspectives. Suggested questions include the following.

    a. On a scale of 1–5 (1 being "I don't handle sudden challenges well" and 5 being "I handle sudden challenges very well"), how do you handle sudden challenges? Why did you give yourself that rating? Can you give an example of how you handle challenges in and out of school?

    b. What strategies do you use to effectively handle challenges you encounter? What other strategies could you use to effectively handle challenges you encounter?

7. Conduct an individual audit of incorporating perspective and perplexity into your units of learning using the checklist in figure 3.8. Then ask yourself these questions.

    a. What revisions did you make from your original unit of learning given the elements of perspective and perplexity?

    b. How do you see these changes impacting students' experience and learning?

    c. How could students be involved in creating perspective- and perplexity-laden experiences in the classroom?

	Tasks	Initial Draft	Revisions
☐ **Perspective**	☐ Refine driving questions to evoke multiple perspectives. ☐ Employ reading, writing, and talking tasks that ensure all voices are heard. ☐ Use specific protocols that ensure all voices are heard.		
☐ **Perplexity**	☐ Change task and criteria expectations. ☐ Change context.		

Figure 3.8: Incorporating perspective and perplexity into units of study.

*Visit **go.SolutionTree.com/instruction** for a free reproducible version of this figure.*

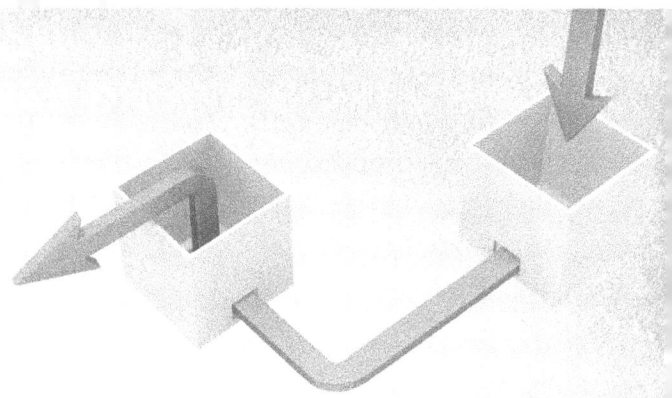

Chapter 4

Engaging Students in Transfer-Level Learning

Keith Jarrett had been handed a mess.
He'd embrace that mess, and it soared.

—TIM HARFORD

In his TED Talk "How Frustration Can Make Us More Creative," Tim Harford (2015) discusses the story of pianist and composer Keith Jarrett, who was scheduled to play a jazz concert at the Cologne Opera House in Germany in 1975. When Jarrett arrived at the concert hall a few hours before his performance, he found that the piano was less than ideal for the show. The white keys were out of tune; the felt had worn away, making an unusual sound. The black keys were sticking. The pedals didn't work, and the piano was simply too small to project the sound needed for the audience to hear the music. Jarrett had been handed what Harford (2015) calls "a little mess"—and ended up playing what many believe to be the greatest jazz concert in history.

Jarrett had to make adjustments to the way he usually played the piano. He had to pound the keys much harder than he usually did when he played jazz. He had to stay away from certain keys because of their atypical sound. He had to adapt to the constraints that were presented to him and in essence destroy his previous means of playing his music and create new ways of conveying his work. He created a masterpiece extemporaneously in front of an entire crowd and made his most beautiful work to date.

There are countless examples of creativity emerging not from willful, strategic planning but due, in large part, to unplanned and unexpected events that people encounter. In his article "The Gift of Doubt," Malcolm Gladwell (2013) discusses the Karnaphuli Paper Mill in East Pakistan, which had been built to make paper out of bamboo. Unfortunately, as the mill opened, a rare incident occurred where the bamboo suddenly flowered and died. Dead bamboo could not be used for pulp, as it simply fell apart as it traveled down the waterways to the mill. But the mill's operators quickly responded by finding new ways to bring bamboo to the mill, creating a new supply chain. Moreover, they discovered new ways to identify and grow different species of bamboo to replace the dead bamboo, and they found different plants to diversify their raw materials.

Keith Jarrett did not want to play the concert at the Cologne Opera House. In fact, he initially left, saying he *wouldn't* play, only to be persuaded by guilt from a young girl pleading with him. The mill's operators weren't looking to create diverse supply chains and research various types of materials. They faced a problem they didn't want to face and took it on because they were already so invested.

German scholar Albert O. Hirschman (as cited in Gladwell, 2013) states:

> Creativity always comes as a surprise to us; therefore we can never count on it and we dare not believe in it until it has happened. In other words, we would not consciously engage upon tasks whose success clearly requires that creativity be forthcoming.

The only way for students to learn the valuable lessons of creativity is to give them the tools and experiences that equip them to handle seemingly routine problems that become more complex and challenging than they originally assumed. By having students use activation skills in their learning when they face challenges, apply transfer skills across contexts, and employ authentic-engagement approaches, they will be well prepared for transfer-level work in the future.

This chapter will cover the key areas of teaching for transfer along with the key success criteria for each student, which are shown in figure 4.1.

The chapter tackles these criteria by focusing on the following three key skills we want students to develop.

1. **Activation:** Strategies that enable students to manage the challenging environment of transfer-level work

2. **Application:** Strategies that enable students to transfer learning from one problem situation to another

3. **Authenticity:** Strategies that enable students to engage with the people, places, and processes in problem-based contexts

In this chapter, we walk through each of these practices to support students in engaging in transfer-level work. First, we will discuss the critical importance of activation for students, a skill discussed in chapter 1 (page 17) that we will revisit in the realm of transfer and that will help students mentally prepare to exercise the two remaining skills. Next, we will look at the skills necessary for students to

Key Areas	Student Success Criteria	Teacher Success Criteria
Comparisons Across Problems Students develop transfer-level skills to engage in transfer-level problems.	Students engage in transfer-level learning by applying their content knowledge and skills via: • Creating analogous problems • Interacting with comparison tasks and contexts • Generating and testing hypotheses	Effective teaching strategies include teaching transfer through: • Presenting analogous situations to students • Providing tools, resources, and instruction that enable students to recognize patterns in and across problems • Providing tools, resources, and instruction that enable students to recognize similarities and differences in problems • Providing tools, resources, and instruction that enable students to act on problems
Community Engagement Students solve impactful problems through the involvement of others.	Students solve transfer-level problems by authentically: • Engaging with communities, audiences, and experts in problem contexts • Engaging in problem-solving processes and protocols to generate solutions for the transfer-level problems	Effective teaching strategies include teaching transfer through: • Creating situations that require students to collect information from people and organizations outside the classroom and school • Providing tools, resources, and explicit instruction that enable students to analyze information from people and organizations outside the classroom and school • Providing tools, resources, and explicit instruction to problem solve with people and organizations outside the classroom and school to generate solutions to transfer-level problems

Figure 4.1: Key areas and success criteria of learning and teaching for transfer.

make comparisons within and between different problems. This notion of application enables students to shift from making connections between different concepts within a single discipline to making connections across disciplines. Finally, we will cover the skills of authenticity—how students can engage with others outside the classroom and school context, as well as use strategies that align with those of experts who solve real-world problems. In the final chapter, we will look at the conditions teachers may create to ensure such practices flourish in the classroom.

Activation: Strategies That Enable Students to Manage the Challenging Environment of Transfer-Level Work

Transfer-level work can be emotionally draining, not necessarily desirable, and highly atypical of the experiences students (and many adults) are familiar with. Though the work may certainly be interesting, there is a high level of failure in transfer work. This can be unsettling for many. As renowned economist John Maynard Keynes (2018) argues, "Worldly wisdom teaches us that it is better for reputation to fail conventionally than to succeed unconventionally" (p. 138). As such, students have to develop a set of skills that allows them to overcome this worldly wisdom and be prepared for the journey required to succeed unconventionally. They must leverage activation skills to experiment in the garage and bring together those spare parts from other disciplines.

Hirschman (as cited in Gladwell, 2013) claims that people are "apt to take on and plunge into new tasks because of the erroneously presumed *absence* of a challenge—because the task looks easier and more manageable than it will turn out to be." Gladwell (2013) elaborates:

> The entrepreneur takes risks but does not see himself as a risk-taker, because he operates under the useful delusion that what he's attempting is not risky. Then, trapped in mid-mountain, people discover the truth—and, because it is too late to turn back, they're forced to finish the job.

Hirschman's and Gladwell's thoughts provide a powerful lesson on creativity and in learning. We create from constraint, which is largely unplanned and unexpected. How, then, do we best prepare students for such work?

The suggestion here is to incorporate routine protocols for developing students' ability to engage in activation-based strategies that are helpful when delving into transfer-level work. Such strategies will enable students to handle constraints, especially when facing the perspective- and perplexity-laden situations outlined in chapter 3 (page 57). Let's examine the following student activation strategies that are impactful at the transfer level.

- ▸ Processing information and planning next steps
- ▸ Giving and receiving feedback
- ▸ Reflecting through action

Processing Information and Planning Next Steps

When students are learning to transfer knowledge and skills, they analyze and evaluate multiple contexts; work to solve problems within one or more of those contexts; often communicate face-to-face with people who offer varied facts, ideas, and opinions; and handle changes and setbacks that emerge during transfer learning. Students need to be able to lay out a problem-solving strategy and effectively engage with peers and people outside the classroom who have ideas different from their own, simultaneously discerning fact from fiction to effectively solve problems, and they need the emotional support to handle changes they will encounter in realistic situations. Figure C.1 in appendix C (page 145) provides a series of specific strategies that you may use to enable students to process information and plan next steps.

Giving and Receiving Feedback

A necessity of engaging in transfer-level learning is for students to receive input into successes and failures along the way. This input should come from multiple sources, including the teacher, other students, and external audiences (for example, a researcher during a videoconference with the class or an expert following the expert's review of a student paper). Students are then obligated to evaluate the feedback and decide what information they will utilize and what they will discard or reject outright. Figure C.2 in appendix C (page 146) provides a series of specific strategies that you may use to enable students to give and receive feedback.

Reflecting Through Action

One key element of handling change and developing resilience is setting the right mindset through the appropriate actions. Behaviors precede beliefs in real life, and students need to focus on actions they can take in the short term (Reeves, 2013). Over time, students learn how to develop certain beliefs through actual experiences in which specific actions require them to realize and handle failure, see different perspectives, and engage in cognitive challenges. In other words, as a teacher, don't spend much time exalting the benefits of a growth mindset; rather, have students focus on the actions that are associated with a growth mindset (Dweck, 2006). Move to action. Teach a growth mindset through experiences you present to students that are constructed in the classroom or depend on students interacting with the real world. You can't really teach students how to handle the last fifty yards of a five-hundred-yard freestyle until they have done the work. Then they reflect on their work, what went well, what didn't go so well, and how they push forward when they naturally want to slow down and rest. A growth mindset is nurtured through action. As such, students should spend more time focusing on their next steps.

We need students to routinely think about what they'll do next after engaging in a challenge to get better. Research, including that of Joshua D. Margolis and Paul G. Stoltz (2010), points to a *response orientation* to a problem. Margolis and Stoltz (2010) describe four lenses people must look through when facing a situation: (1) control, (2) impact, (3) breadth, and (4) duration (see table 4.1, page 78). Those who take a response-oriented approach focus on what elements they can control right now to improve the situation, what level of impact they can have now to improve the situation, and how they can enhance or limit the breadth or duration of the situation. Often, people who struggle with taking immediate action also struggle with taking a proactive response orientation and instead approach problem solving from a *cause orientation*. These individuals are deeply reflective and spend more time defining and describing the problem. Obviously, understanding root causes and reflecting on challenging situations can be helpful, but the balance of deep reflection should be equal to or less than a response orientation to problems.

Table 4.1 illustrates key differences between cause-oriented and response-oriented thinking and the four lenses students can use to evaluate situations and plan appropriate actions. See figure C.4 in appendix C (page 147) for a series of specific strategies that teachers may use to enable students to reflect and connect.

Table 4.1: Shifting From Reflective Cause-Oriented Thinking to Active Response-Oriented Thinking

Lens	Cause-Oriented Thinking	Response-Oriented Thinking
Control	Was this adverse event inevitable, or could I have prevented it?	What features of the situation can I (even potentially) improve?
Impact	Did I cause this adverse event, or did it result from external sources?	What sort of positive impact can I have on what's next?
Breadth	Is the underlying event specific to the situation, or is it more widespread?	How can I contain the negatives of the situation and generate currently unseen positives?
Duration	Is the underlying event enduring or temporary?	What can I do to begin addressing the problem now?

Application: Strategies That Enable Students to Transfer Learning From One Problem Situation to Another

One of the key goals of transfer is for students to apply surface and deep knowledge to a new problem within or across disciplines. To help develop this skill in our students, we must first understand one of the classic examples of applying knowledge across contexts.

A number of studies in the 1980s illustrated the challenges adults face when attempting to apply ideas across contexts. For example, in one study, researchers Mary L. Gick and Keith J. Holyoak (1980) asked participants to solve Karl Duncker's (1945) radiation problem. Review this problem in figure 4.2, and attempt to solve it.

Suppose you are a doctor faced with a patient who has a malignant tumor in his stomach. It is impossible to operate on the patient, but unless the tumor is destroyed the patient will die. There is a kind of ray that can be used to destroy the tumor. If the rays reach the tumor all at once at a sufficiently high intensity, the tumor will be destroyed. Unfortunately, at this intensity the healthy tissue that the rays pass through on the way to the tumor will also be destroyed. At lower intensities the rays are harmless to healthy tissue, but they will not affect the tumor either.

What type of procedure might be used to destroy the tumor with the rays, and at the same time avoid destroying the healthy tissue?

Source: Gick & Holyoak, 1980, pp. 307–308.

Figure 4.2: The radiation problem.

Gick and Holyoak (1980) found that if you simply have people read the radiation problem, about 10 percent of people can solve the problem. However, when presented with another problem (see the commander problem in figure 4.3), about 30 percent see the underlying pattern between the problems and thus solve the problem. Interestingly, more than 70 percent of people do not inherently see the connection between the problems and therefore can't solve the problem (Gick & Holyoak, 1983).

A small country was ruled from a strong fortress by a dictator. The fortress was situated in the middle of the country, surrounded by farms and villages. Many roads led to the fortress through the countryside. A rebel general vowed to capture the fortress. The general knew that an attack by his entire army would capture the fortress. He gathered his army at the head of one of the roads, ready to launch a full-scale direct attack. However, the general then learned that the dictator had planted mines on each of the roads. The mines were set so that small bodies of men could pass over them safely, since the dictator needed to move his troops and workers to and from the fortress. However, any large force would detonate the mines. This would not only blow up the road but destroy many neighboring villages. It therefore seemed impossible to capture the fortress.

The general, however, devised a simple plan. He positioned a small detachment of soldiers at the head of different roads, and on his order they marched along different roads to the fortress and arrived at the same time, thereby overthrowing the dictator.

Source: Adapted from Gick & Holyoak, 1980.

Figure 4.3: The commander problem.

The researchers didn't stop there. When given a third problem (see the fire problem in figure 4.4, page 80), about 50 percent solve the problem (Gick & Holyoak, 1983).

> Years ago, a small-town fire chief arrived at a woodshed fire, concerned that it would spread to a nearby house if it was not extinguished quickly. There was no hydrant nearby, but the shed was next to a lake, so there was plenty of water. Dozens of neighbors were already taking turns with buckets throwing water on the shed, but they weren't making any progress. The neighbors were surprised when the fire chief yelled at them to stop, and to all go fill their buckets in the lake. When they returned, the chief arranged them in a circle around the shed, and on the count of three had them all throw their water at once. The fire was immediately dampened, and soon thereafter extinguished. The town gave the fire chief a pay raise as a reward for quick thinking.

Source: Epstein, 2019, p. 105.

Figure 4.4: The fire problem.

As Epstein (2019) explains, "A gift of a single analogy from a different domain tripled the proportion of solvers who got the radiation problem. Two analogies from disparate domains gave an even bigger boost" (p. 106). Interestingly, most people do not utilize these analogies until directed to do so. Our brains, after countless hours of focusing on surface-and-deep networks, are set up for problems that repeat and conditions that are controlled. We struggle with thinking across boxes and leveraging analogies to solve problems that are outside surface-and-deep networks.

How do we reconcile this challenge in the classroom? Gick and Holyoak (1980, 1983) provide a simple solution: offering subtle suggestions that two seemingly disparate stories actually relate (that is, comparing the radiation and the commander contexts) will help people answer the question. When they do this, 80 percent of participants are able to see the relationship between the various stories and the radiation problem. Put another way, with a gentle nudge, participants are usually able to spot the *underlying structure* of the problem and not be blinded by the *contexts*. The challenge is that teachers will not always be able to cue students when transfer-level thinking is needed. Moreover, even when students develop an awareness that such thinking is needed, students may lack the specific skills to transfer learning across contexts.

John Hattie and Gregory M. Donoghue (2016) find that transfer learning is fundamentally a student's ability to detect the differences and similarities between two or more situations and to see patterns between problems. Reviewing a synthesis of literature that encompassed a sample size of approximately thirteen thousand students, Hattie and Donoghue (2016) illustrate that providing students with the tools and intentional instruction to recognize similarities, differences, and patterns across problems is, perhaps, the most effective strategy to teach for transfer learning. Table 4.2 shows the number of studies, the number of people, and the net effect size of two transfer-level strategies on student learning. Please note that an effect size of .40 is approximately the equivalent of one year's growth in one year's time (Hattie, 2009).

Table 4.2: Effect Size of Transfer-Level Strategies

Transfer	Number of Studies	Prorated Number of People	Effect Size
Similarities and differences	51	13,300	1.32
Seeing patterns to new situations	6	13,300	1.14

Source: Adapted from Hattie & Donoghue, 2016.

Given the studies we have reviewed, consider the following highly recommended application strategies for developing transfer skills.

▸ Comparing contexts

▸ Creating analogous problems

Of course, developing the skills to detect the similarities and differences between situations, or seeing patterns to new situations, does not require students to take action. The garage is about not only building and creating something but putting those new innovations to use. Therefore, we need a strategy that requires lateral thinking and a call to action. Marzano (2017) argues for the use of generating and testing hypotheses as a core strategy for understanding various situations and doing something with that knowledge. As such, we will add generating and testing hypotheses to our transfer toolbox.

Comparing Contexts

One of the most powerful ways of developing transfer-level networks is to compare problem contexts. Dedre Gentner and her collaborators (as cited in Willingham, 2018) have tried (with some success) to improve transfer skills by prompting students to separate the contexts from the underlying structure that both problems share. Hattie and Donoghue (2016) quantify "some success" by showing that after analyzing more than fifty studies, the effect size of analyzing similarities and differences between problems is equivalent to more than two years' growth in one year's time. As shown in the Gick and Holyoak (1980, 1983) studies, enabling students to separate the context from the content enables a greater ability to transfer. Moreover, in chapter 1 (page 17), we discussed the power of clarity of learning intentions and success criteria relative to tasks and contexts. Put together, the power of clarity is essential for student growth in learning across levels of complexity (Hattie, 2009). One way to think of comparison problems is in relation to spot-the-difference puzzles, which require people to find a set of differences between two otherwise similar images.

Let's look at the spot-the-difference approach with a classic near-transfer problem in mathematics: the infamous two trains heading at each other, or the first rate problem from figure 2.11 in chapter 2 (page 47). Suppose we have two trains leaving different cities heading toward each other at different speeds. When do the two trains meet? How far from each city do they meet? To enable students to transfer their learning, we would give them a second problem—the second rate problem from figure 2.11. Two boats are leaving different cities and heading toward each other at different speeds. When do the two boats meet? How far from each city do they meet?

By having students evaluate both problem situations and then identify the similarities and differences between the problems, they have a higher likelihood of solving not one or both problems but multiple problems, effectively transferring their knowledge across situations. Table 4.3 illustrates the similarities and differences between the two mathematical problems.

Table 4.3: Comparison Example of Two Contexts in Mathematics

	Boat Situation	**Train Situation**
Similarities	Requires the same operations distance / rate = time distance / time = rate	Requires the same operations distance / rate = time distance / time = rate
Differences	Context (boat versus train) Unit of speed (knots versus mph) Quantities (differences in rate, time, and distance)	Context (train versus boat) Unit of speed (mph versus knots) Quantities (differences in rate, time, and distance)

There are multiple ways to support students in spotting differences or comparing problems. This book highlights three: (1) perspective analysis across contexts, (2) entry events, and (3) exemplar comparisons.

Perspective Analysis Across Contexts

A number of classroom-based strategies enable students to see similarities and differences between and across problems (see figure 4.5, page 84). Marzano (1992) illustrates the power of *perspective analysis* as a tool to identify multiple opposing positions on one specific topic. See figure B.5 (page 143) in appendix B for a detailed step-by-step approach for having students analyze different perspectives. In chapter 3 (page 57), we discussed the importance of exposing students to different perspectives as a means to confront change. Here, we go a little further, using strategies that ask students to analyze perspectives across multiple contexts and to discuss similarities and differences that emerge across contexts from these perspectives.

For example, let's imagine students read the book *A Tale of Two Beasts* by Fiona Roberton (2013). The book presents two stories, each from a different perspective. The first is told from the perspective of a little girl who rescues a strange beast—a squirrel—in the woods and safely carries him home. The second story is told from the perspective of the squirrel, who explains how a strange beast—the little girl— took him. As discussed in chapter 3 (page 57), changing perspective is incredibly powerful for supporting students in moving from deep to transfer learning. The distinct difference here is to illustrate for students multiple perspectives across multiple contexts—having them consider the wolf's perspective in *The Three Little Pigs*, analyze the play *Wicked* alongside *The Wizard of Oz*, view Aaron Burr as a protagonist rather than an antagonist in *Hamilton*, compare Grendel to Beowulf, and so forth.

Entry Events

One way to prepare students for transfer-level work is to *start* a unit of study at the transfer level. One way to do this is to provide an entry event. An entry event is an experience at the beginning of a unit in which students determine the driving question, identify the learning intentions and success criteria, and co-create the steps required to answer the driving question. For example, earlier in the book, we discussed how teachers may present antipoaching efforts in Mozambique and the marine-mammal rescue-and-rehabilitation challenges in Marin County. Imagine that a teacher launches the unit of study with these two contexts. The teacher then provides students with news articles or research studies on each context and then asks students to create the driving question—for example, "To what extent should the government of Mozambique ensure the protection of an important resource for international tourism and general national interests while balancing the economic disparities in and around Maputo?" Next, the teacher may ask students to identify the learning intentions, success criteria, and what they need to learn to address the driving question.

Figure 4.5 (page 84) illustrates a number of contexts that students could compare and contrast and perspectives they could identify.

Exemplar Comparisons

If we were to take a step back and think about ourselves as students in a K–12 classroom, we would most likely agree that knowing what success looks like is a sure-fire way for us to meet our classroom teacher's expectations. The challenge inevitably is that if we are given the exact blueprint of success, how will we ensure that we are not copying the example verbatim but rather inspecting the criteria that make the example so successful?

One way to support students in seeing the actual attributes of success is to provide them with different samples of ideal success in different contexts. This allows students to identify the key criteria for success and makes it less likely for them to get hung up on the context. Let's say, for example, that students are expected to write an informational essay on habitats. The teacher may provide students with multiple examples of successful informational essays—in which none of the exemplars are related to habitats. Moreover, the successful examples may cover a range of topics (for example, ice cream flavors, school uniforms, and health care reform).

Another option would be to give students different levels of performance expectations, which allows students to identify typical progressions students go through from initial drafting to a finished product. This helps students better understand the

	Steroids in Sports	**Boston Tea Party**	*Gladiator* **Podcast**	**Iran-Contra Affair**
Context	A swimmer has been caught using a particular steroid to enable quicker recovery time from a back injury that required surgery. The swimmer has been banned from competing in the summer Olympics.	Recent research has shown that those involved in the Boston Tea Party were throwing tea into the harbor not for political reasons but to limit the supply of tea in Boston to increase their personal revenue.	The powerful narrative of Aaron Hernandez illustrates the violence of football and the pressure on players and coaches.	During the Iran-Contra Affair, the U.S. public predominantly received information from the news and their government that illustrated the United States was making sound and responsible decisions.
Key Question	Should athletes be able to use steroids if they are recovering from injury, or is this cheating?	To what extent did Boston Tea Party participants engage in a display of political conflict versus a purely economic one?	How do we reconcile brain injury with the financial gains and popularity of American football?	Should we provide one perspective to a group of people when a nation is at war?
Perspective 1	I'm open to the use of steroids for recovery purposes.	I'm closed to these findings, as they contradict other sources of information.	Players should be able to choose. They should know the risks and then decide what they want to do.	I'm interested only in information from my government and news agencies from my country.
Perspective 2	I'm closed to the use of steroids for recovery purposes.	I'm open to these findings because of the reliability and validity of the sources.	Football should be banned as a sport.	I'm interested in information from multiple governments and news agencies from other countries.
Perspective 3	I'm neutral on the use of steroids in athletics.	I'm undecided and looking for additional information.	We should maintain the status quo. Little can be done, and what has already been done is about the best we can do.	I'm undecided on my comfort level or interest in looking at multiple perspectives.

Figure 4.5: Comparing contexts and perspectives.

learning expectations. Students typically interact with peers to determine success, rank exemplars, and debate on improving pieces of work.

Though exemplars may be used at any time of instruction, they are very helpful at the beginning of the learning sequence. When teachers provide students with exemplars up front, students can interact with what success looks like from the start of the unit of instruction. Moreover, this gives teachers an opportunity to preassess where students are in their performance and co-construct expectations for student learning, which aids students in increasing clarity, assessing their own work, and giving and receiving feedback.

Creating Analogous Problems

In addition to providing students with multiple contexts to compare, having students create their own analogous problems can be incredibly helpful in seeing patterns within and between problems and therefore developing transfer networks. For example, psychologists Ricardo A. Minervino, Valeria Olguín, and Máximo Trench (2017) found that when subjects were asked to read the commander problem and then create an analogous problem of their own design, they were more likely to solve the radiation problem than those subjects who were not asked to create a problem (see figure 4.6). Creating analogies allowed subjects to see the recurring themes or patterns within and across problems. Whereas comparison problems most effectively support detecting the contextual differences, analogous problems enable students to better recognize patterns within and across problems.

In the study by Minervino and colleagues (2017), those subjects who created better analogies to the initial problem—that is, the commander problem—proved to be the most effective in solving the radiation problem. But creating an analogy to solve one problem in one context is simply not that effective. In the study, participants who created an analogy by looking at only one context (for example, the commander problem) did no better than those individuals who compared two contexts without an analogy (Minervino et al., 2017).

As such, having students compare different examples across contexts before creating an analogy appears necessary for students to transfer. Figure 4.6 illustrates five analogies participants generated after they reviewed the commander problem.

---

1. The entire town was planning a protest against a sudden raise in the price of electricity. A prolonged and total interruption of consumption would make the company prone to rethinking the appropriateness of the price hike. However, not using any electricity would involve threats to security, as well as the loss of refrigerated food.

2. A patient had a severe infection that needed to be controlled in less than an hour. A certain kind of antibiotic could potentially control it, if an extreme dosage of it were immediately channeled into the blood flow. The problem was that injecting such an amount of antibiotic through any particular vessel would irreversibly damage it.

3. A pair of pants was stained with ink. The ink spot could be removed by a solution of chlorine of the sufficient concentration. The problem was that a solution of the required concentration would also bleach the area surrounding the spot.

4. A car had fallen into a deep pit. Even though there were tow trucks that had sufficient strength to lift the car, attaching the tow to any single part of the chassis would break that part.

5. A scuba diver got locked inside a wreck and needed to be rescued immediately. A team of five professional divers would suffice to take him out of the wreck. However, that number of divers swimming together would arouse the attention of sharks.

Source: Adapted from Minervino et al., 2017.

Figure 4.6: Analogous examples from the commander transfer problem.

Table 4.4 illustrates four strategies that support students in comparing exemplars and enable them to see similarities and differences as well as notice patterns across problems. See figure C.5 in appendix C (page 148) for detailed information on each strategy.

Table 4.4: Creating Analogous Problems

Strategy	Description
Sentence-stem analogies	Ask students to create sentence-stem analogies for abstract concepts or ideas.
Visual analogies	Ask students to create alternative ways to express analogies visually.
Metaphors	Instruct students to make a comparison.
Similes	Invite students to make a comparison between two subjects using *like* or *as*.

Generating and Testing Hypotheses

Beyond comparing contexts and creating analogous problems, generating and testing hypotheses is an effective strategy for enabling students to transfer learning. Here, students are required to explain their hypotheses, investigate their logical guesses, and make conclusions. Following are three examples of typical questions teachers might ask in the classroom.

1. What is your hypothesis as to the best method for ending World War II other than the use of the atomic bomb? How will you test your hypothesis?

2. If you were president of the United States during World War II, how would you have forced the unconditional surrender of Japan without using the atomic bomb yet provided for a secure postwar world?

3. Why did Japan attack Pearl Harbor? Some say President Roosevelt intentionally provoked the Japanese, and others disagree. What is your hypothesis? Collect evidence that confirms your hypothesis.

Questions associated with transfer include the following three examples.

1. To what extent does your hypothesis for ending World War II apply to America's decision to step away from the Iran nuclear deal? How will you test your hypothesis? How does your hypothesis apply to internal conflicts in business or staff meetings?

2. Based on your hypothesis related to question 2 in the previous list, how would you handle a merger between two companies in order to maintain a strong market position and brand recognition? What conditions would you evaluate to change or maintain your hypothesis? How would you test your hypothesis in this context?

3. Based on your hypothesis related to question 3 in the previous list, how would you test whether your hypothesis applies to the more contemporary inference that gun violence is escalating because of partisan rhetoric about immigration and diversity? Collect evidence that confirms or rejects your hypothesis.

Marzano (2017) offers the following question for teachers to consider: *What will I do to help students generate and test hypotheses about new knowledge?* Robert J. Marzano, Debra J. Pickering, and Jane E. Pollock (2001) argue that there are two main entry points to generating and testing hypotheses: (1) deductive thinking and (2) inductive thinking.

According to Marzano and colleagues (2001), "Deductive thinking is the process of using a general rule to make a prediction" (p. 104). For example, students may hypothesize how they may use certain rules in sports, such as those that bar steroid use, to test new situations that emerge in the field of athletics. Inductive thinking starts from the particulars of the situation and, based on information within the field, draws a new conclusion or general rule. In other words, "inductive thinking . . . is the process of drawing new conclusions based on information we know or are presented with" (Marzano et al., 2001, pp. 104–105). For example, students look at specific cases of steroid use, including individuals who are using steroids to recover from injury as opposed to those who are using them for purely competitive advantages. They form hypotheses based on these cases and then test their hypotheses against standard cases in the field (see table 4.5, page 88).

Though not an exhaustive list, the strategies described in table 4.5 (page 88) are sound research-based approaches to best support students in comparing and contrasting problems in similar (that is, near-transfer) contexts and seemingly disparate (that is, far-transfer) contexts. These strategies also help students see patterns within such problems and bring surface and deep knowledge and skills to bear to thoughtfully solve problems. Often, this work requires significant feedback, constant course correction, flipping back and forth from surface and deep thinking to transfer thinking, and switching from one context to another. Preparing students for such work requires intensive support in enabling them to handle change over time.

Of course, transfer-level work and the strategies that enable transfer-level learning do not exist *only*—or, for that matter, *really*—in the classroom and in fact exist squarely outside the classroom with real people, real places, and real problems. This leads to the need for authenticity in transfer-level learning, in which students learn to solve real issues affecting real people outside their classrooms.

Table 4.5: Strategies for Generating and Testing Hypotheses

Strategy	Description
Generate problems of practice and theories of action.	Students follow a step-by-step process (shown in the following numbered list) to identify a problem, create a hypothesis, and test the hypothesis. Students determine challenges (or problems of practice) within a context or contexts. Next, students draft a theory of action, which requires them to create *if–then* statements indicating a hypothesis (the *if*) and the impact of that hypothesis (*then*). Finally, they test their theory of action. 1. Describe a situation that needs attention. 2. Identify the type of problem. 3. Brainstorm ideas and hypothesize what might work. 4. Create prototypes. 5. Test hypotheses with prototypes. 6. Revise hypotheses or prototypes based on findings.
Engage in a decision-making process.	Students determine a problem-solving or decision-making process that will enable them to test their hypotheses.
Provide grounds, backing, and qualifiers to support claims.	Students qualify their findings to support or reject their hypotheses.
Find and correct errors or limitations in claims.	Students identify errors of attack: ask students to compose or find examples of errors in defending or rejecting a side of an issue. Students challenge weak references: ask students to compose or find examples of errors of weak reference. Students find errors of misinformation in information. Students inspect logical fallacies, statistical limitations, and ad hominem attacks that relate to their hypotheses.
Engage in critical review of solutions.	Students compare their or their group's approach to a problem with another student's or group's approach to the same problem.
Test hypotheses.	• Provide templates for reporting, with areas for students' explanations. • Offer sentence stems to help students develop their explanations. • Encourage the use of audio or video recording for explaining hypotheses and conclusions. • Provide rubrics and exemplars. • Invite an audience for students' presentation of hypotheses or conclusions.

Authenticity: Strategies That Enable Students to Engage With the People, Places, and Processes in Problem-Based Contexts

There is a moment in the musical *Hamilton* where Aaron Burr, the antagonist, finds out Alexander Hamilton, the protagonist, has the opportunity to negotiate with James Madison and Thomas Jefferson on a policy to establish the first federal bank of the United States of America. Throughout the musical, Burr plays every situation as safely as possible. He keeps a safe distance from danger and is methodical in every move to advance his social, political, and economic standings. Alexander Hamilton is the opposite, taking chances and risking his actual life and any and all capital to make a name for himself and make a difference in forming a new nation.

During the song "The Room Where It Happens" (Miranda, 2015), Hamilton capitulates and agrees with Burr that he must compromise to get things done, ensuring the federal bank gets approved (that is, talk less and smile more). Interestingly, Burr is the one who has stayed on the sidelines his whole life and as a result is left waiting outside the negotiations. He certainly brings sound advice to bear, but he doesn't get a chance to take part in the important decisions that shape early America. He is a critic who wants the fanfare of the arena but not the blood, sweat, and tears that it takes to make decisions.

Teachers want to ensure that students are "in the room where it happens"—that they get to take part in and shape decisions that affect the future. As such, students need to be in the arena, not on the sidelines, in order to build and solidify transfer networks. In order for students to take part in authentic work, teachers must ensure students are engaging with communities, audiences, and experts—or working on real-world tasks with people who are impacted by or working on those tasks—as well as incorporating transfer-level strategies when problem solving so that there's a high level of integrity to the solutions they propose.

Engaging With Communities, Audiences, and Experts

In the application section of this chapter, we discussed strategies for students to compare contexts, create analogous problems, and generate and test hypotheses. In this section on authenticity, we are looking at how to employ those same strategies, but with people in real-world contexts. Students must be able to transition from the lab to the field. They need to interact with and present to others in one or more contexts. This includes:

▸ Engaging with people who are impacted by problems and people who are researching the problems

▸ Collecting and using evidence within the context to inform decisions

▸ Sharing findings on the utility of ideas and preparing for feedback

▸ Collecting information from several sources

There are myriad ways of engaging with people outside the classroom context, including field trips, virtual one-on-one meetings, panel discussions, and recorded audio interviews. In one class, I had students use Skype to interview researchers on honeybee conservation. Students devised a number of questions on colony collapse disorder and posed them to professors and biologists all over the world. A second-grade group scheduled a virtual meeting with a large team at Google to discuss ways in which the company uses Google Earth to assist governments, organizations, and citizens in overcoming logistical challenges. Other opportunities might include inviting a novelist to class to discuss how the writer develops a story, convening a panel of nurses and doctors to listen in and offer feedback on student proposals, visiting a community impacted by eminent domain ordinances, and creating a podcast related to the most effective forensic techniques for cases involving ballistics. Before organizing such activities, you should check your school's or district's policy on permission for engaging with those outside the school. Usually, with just a bit of paperwork, you can have your students working with experts and community members in no time.

Figure 4.7 shows some strategies to help students engage with communities, audiences, and experts.

Strategy	Description	Example
Interviews	Students ask individuals and groups a series of questions to understand perspectives and problems.	Students go into a community center (a church, a local restaurant, or an organization such as an Elks Lodge or Lions Club) and ask questions related to a community issue (for example, gun control or birth control) and write down or record all the information from others.
Presentations	Students deliver project progress solutions through an oral presentation.	Students deliver a presentation on their findings to a group of community leaders, professionals, classmates, and the teacher.
Storytelling	Students utilize anecdotes, metaphors, and analogies that connect key themes and topics to real-life stories.	Students tell a story about one of the interviewees to reinforce their key ideas.
Empathy Protocols	Students go through specific routines to understand other people's perspectives.	Students ask a series of questions to understand the perspectives of people outside the classroom (for example, individuals impacted by a specific issue or who have expertise in a specific field).

Figure 4.7: Strategies for engaging with communities, audiences, and experts.

Incorporating Transfer-Level Strategies When Problem Solving

Students need a process for using the information collected from other people to create a workable solution while not falling into the biases inherent in surface-and-deep networks (see table 4.6). Students must make decisions that are akin to those of experts who engage in transfer-level work and that are useful to those impacted by the problem context. Typically, students default to routine problem-solving thinking, relying on their surface- and deep-level knowledge rather than the lateral transfer-level thinking required. This is a problem not just for novices but for experts. Researcher Pedro Domingos (as cited in Epstein, 2019) writes, "Knowledge is a double-edged sword. It allows you to do some things, but it also makes you blind to other things that you could do" (p. 179). Psychology professor Victor Ottati (as cited in Robson, 2019) calls this myopic focus on surface and deep knowledge "earned dogmatism"—and it prohibits experts from looking broadly and instead supports opaque filters that focus on depth (p. 71). That is, they take a narrow view of the problem and lack the ability to think broadly, across contexts. Study after study has shown that people fail to transfer learning across disciplines, even when they possess core knowledge and skills in different disciplines, because they fail to compare (Epstein, 2019).

Table 4.6: Comparing Approaches to Problem Solving

Surface and Deep Approaches to Problem Solving	Transfer Approaches to Problem Solving
Focus on internal details of *one* situation.	Focus on similarities and differences between situations.
When prompted, only look at comparison situations that are closely aligned with the situation at hand.	Look at comparison situations that may have a distant relationship with the situation at hand.
Be overconfident in your understanding of the situation and rely on intuition and expertise within that situation.	Use inquiry to test assumptions of your understanding of a situation.
Determine the solution and evaluate the problem later.	Start with problem types before jumping to solutions—and look at an array of solutions before selecting a solution.
Engage in groupthink with other experts.	Engage with others outside of areas of expertise.

For example, in the early 1980s, author Paul Nutt (2002) cataloged the real-world decision-making approaches of more than seventy different U.S. organizations. Of the cases Nutt studied, only 15 percent of organizations actually sought out an alternative from the original solution posed by the organization. Even more surprisingly, only 29 percent considered an alternative beyond dichotomous *either–or* options. That is, 71 percent of organizations never weighed a third option to their long-term decision making (Nutt, 2002). Those decision-making processes that did not involve lateral thinking resulted in faulty products, lack of creative development, and customer and community dissatisfaction.

Let's look at another example. Two groups of Stanford students were given a scenario in which they had to find an appropriate response for how to support a small fictional democratic country under threat from a totalitarian neighbor. One group of students received the following information: the president of the country was originally from New York, there were refugees in boxcars, and students were to meet in Winston Churchill Hall. The second group was told that the president of the country was originally from Texas, the "same state as LBJ," and that refugees were in boats (Epstein, 2019, p. 107).

Interestingly, the first group stated that the best approach was to engage in war, whereas the second group believed that a diplomatic resolution was most appropriate. Both groups were encumbered by the contextual information. The first group thought only of World War II, whereas the second group thought of Vietnam. What if the groups actually stepped out of their specific situations and analyzed different business ventures (for example, potential monopoly), looked at different wars (for example, Vietnam, World War II, and Iraq), studied animal behaviors (such as commensalism, mutualism, and parasitism), and then determined a solution?

To transition from our default mode of thinking in the world of routines and consistent patterns to the transfer-level thinking required in the world of ill-defined problems, students need new ways of thinking. The default is to double down on knowledge. Transfer involves leveraging curiosity. When you have both knowledge and inquiry, you have found the bliss of meaningful innovation. Perhaps when we leave the world of the routine, we find that we encounter the world of counterintuition, delay, and frustration. But these experiences are necessary not just for learning but for engaging in transfer-level knowledge and skill development.

To do this, students must identify methods of problem solving or decision making to best understand the problem, identify criteria for a solution, draft potential solutions, select a solution, and implement and inspect the delivery of the solution. Moreover, students need to engage in routines that enable them to identify solutions that may have worked in other situations, modify existing solutions to a problem, or invent an entirely new solution. Therefore, students need practice in transferring and modifying ideas (see figure 4.8). The next chapter walks through problem-solving processes, but students must establish strategies for problem solving first. This is what figure 4.8 highlights.

Strategy	Description	Example
Experimental-Inquiry Tasks	Students examine problem-solving and decision-making processes of other researchers, businesses, and nonprofit entities. Next, they use one of those processes to conduct their own work and then compare that process with other processes.	Ask students to utilize the design thinking process out of Stanford's design school to solve a problem (Hasso Plattner Institute of Design at Stanford University, 2020). Next, have students compare that process and their outcomes with total quality management (George, Rowlands, Price, & Maxey, 2005; Liker, 2004). Students then reflect on the differences and potential changes in outcomes.

Third-Option Routines	Students determine solutions to problems and then present a third or alternative solution to the one or two solutions that they determined were the most effective for the problem at hand. Next, students discuss with others why they stuck with or changed their original decision. Often during this process, students are presented with hypothetical changes to the situation—new stakeholders, new variables, new context—and must determine which option most effectively meets those challenges. This stress test allows students to determine the best solution and whether the third option becomes the best one.	Ask students to present two solutions to a problem before a panel of students and staff. The panel immediately asks students to draft a third option that meets the success criteria and meets stakeholder expectations within the problem context. Next, the panel asks students to determine whether the solutions could or would cross to other contexts. Then the panel gives the students a series of hypothetical scenarios and asks them to evaluate the efficacy of their options. Finally, the students present and defend or reject their solution.
Search Paths for Shared Interests	Students are required to meet with stakeholders who are diametrically opposed to one another's positions in a problem situation. They must analyze other situations that have had similar vitriol on both sides and how resolutions came about or fell through. Then, students must develop solutions that most effectively meet both sides of a position by identifying solutions that align with shared interests.	Students meet with stakeholders from two or more groups around a similar issue. They ask each group to identify interests that all groups agree with and the differences in positions. They continue to engage in this process until all groups have been interviewed. Next, students create a shared-interest outline and identify potential solutions that would meet the expectations of all parties. Finally, students receive feedback from all parties.
Future Forecasts	Students forecast an ideal future and discuss what steps they need to take to meet such expectations.	Students produce a series of solutions and steps that would potentially meet their ideal outcome. Students formulate how these solutions would work and evaluate the solutions generated to the extent that they meet the ideal outcomes.
Skunk Works	Students are given current problems and current solutions and then asked to find different problems and different solutions.	Originally the name of a division within aerospace company Lockheed Martin, *Skunk Works* has come to refer to a small group's innovative undertaking that operates outside the normal research-and-development channels within an organization. In the classroom, students take learning intentions and success criteria, determine potential problems, and create solutions to those problems.
Red Team	The following protocol is designed to specifically stress-test a student's or students' solution to a problem. One or more students present the problem context(s) and the solution to a small group of people who then find multiple ways in which the solution will not work and what changes need to be made.	Ask students to present their solution to a small group of students known as the red team. The red team then gives feedback on the solution.

Figure 4.8: Strategies for incorporating transfer-level strategies when problem solving.

Conclusion

To prepare for transfer, students need to manage ambiguity and face setbacks (activation), use knowledge and skills that allow them to see across and understand the relationship between problems (application), and engage with others in the real world (authenticity). This is a far cry from the consistent, routine world of the office. The garage requires students to drop their familiar tools of consistency—to stop hyperfocusing on one area and relying on only the information from their teacher. In the next chapter, we'll explore the specific ideal classroom conditions that enable transfer-level work to unfold.

Reflection Questions

The following questions are designed for you to address individually or in teams to determine the next steps that you will take in the classroom. When you review these questions, it is important that you reflect on the tools you currently use with students and where you may discover tension between your current beliefs and practices and what I've proposed. Educators usually carry with them a set of tools that work well in certain situations. This chapter's contents may have been somewhat familiar to those teachers who have tools that work well in the garage. Teachers who come with a set of tools suited to the office, however, may have found this chapter challenging. Regardless of where you stand, this is an opportunity for you to incorporate new tools.

1. What elements of teaching for transfer—activation, application, and authenticity—seem to be the most doable for you to engage in with students? Why do these steps seem the most possible? What next steps will you take to move toward implementation?

    a. Activation

        i. Processing information and planning next steps

        ii. Giving and receiving feedback

        iii. Reflecting through action

    b. Application

        i. Comparing contexts

        ii. Creating analogous problems

        iii. Generating and testing hypotheses

    c. Authenticity

        i. Engaging with communities, audiences, and experts

        ii. Incorporating transfer-level strategies when problem solving

2. What elements of teaching for transfer seem to be the most challenging for you to engage in with students? Why? What next steps will you take to move toward implementation?

Next Steps

As with the reflection questions, please go through each of these steps individually or as a team and determine what actions you will take in your classroom.

1. Conduct the commander-problem scenario with your grade-level or department team (see figure 4.3; page 79). First, present the commander problem to teachers and ask them to create analogies to it and share their analogies with one another. Next, ask teachers to come up with the core message or repeating pattern from each of the analogies. Then, give teachers the radiation problem (figure 4.2, page 79) and ask that they solve the problem given what they know. Have them discuss the similarities and differences between the commander problem and the radiation problem, and have teachers explain how analogies were helpful in their ability to see the common patterns in both problems and how this supports transfer. Finally, ask teachers to brainstorm ways they could use the same process with students.

2. Have teachers review the strategies in figure 4.7 (page 90) and figure 4.8 (page 92) to identify strategies they will attempt in their own classrooms or within department meetings. After implementation, have teachers reflect on their key learning from engaging with others and expanding their approaches to problem solving and decision making.

3. Draft multiple analogous situations for students to engage with at the beginning of the learning sequence. Students should be directed to see similarities and differences between problems and identify common patterns across problems.

4. Identify one activation, one application, and one authenticity strategy that students will utilize during the next unit of learning.

5. Provide students with the resources to engage with an external audience to better understand and solve real-world problems.

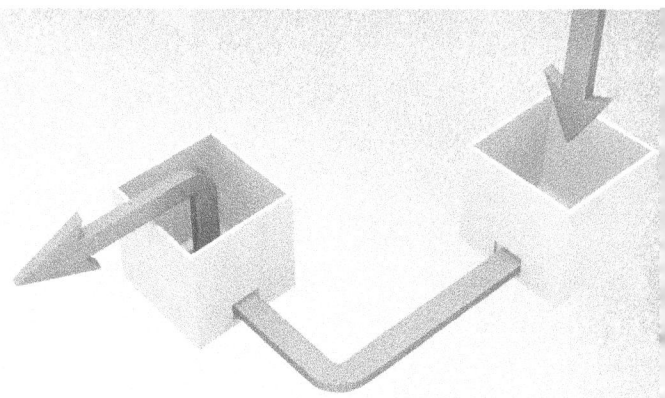

Chapter 5

Integrating Transfer Into Our Teaching and Learning Practices

*Wholeness is not achieved by cutting off a portion of
one's being, but by integration of the contraries.*

—CARL JUNG

According to journalist Liana Simstrom (2019), there is a great deal we can
learn from grasshoppers—namely that they adapt their behavior based on
the situation they are facing. Under normal conditions, they are skittish and
hop away from other grasshoppers. However, when resources are scarce, they band
together. Their behavior shifts given their situation. Humans have had a difficult
time handling this finding. From researcher Michael Anstey's viewpoint (as cited in
Simstrom, 2019), this is due to our inability to believe that our behavior or that of
others shifts in different situations.

We tend to believe that we don't change—that we are the same regardless of what
we face—and this has countless ramifications for people in business, education, and
society. Consider the classic dichotomy that physicist Safi Bahcall (2019) articulates:
some people are artists, who develop new ideas (for example, making the first film
in a franchise), and some people are soldiers, who follow the artists' formulas (for
example, creating the film sequels). Artists, the dreamers and inventors, stick to the
world of transfer learning, and the soldiers, who carry out orders and refine processes,
remain in the world of surface and deep learning.

As we have discussed throughout this book, students must develop surface and deep
and transfer knowledge and skills. There is a time for students to be like soldiers—
performing procedures, following routines, and the like. This is fitting for instances

in which problems are clearly defined, widely understood, and easily replicated. However, when problems are ill defined, students must be more like artists— exploring the boundaries of disciplines, seeking new processes, and so forth. Sometimes, students are in the office accomplishing routine tasks, and other times, they must do away with routines. There is a time and a place for surface, deep, and transfer learning, and students must be prepared for the integration of all three. Like grasshoppers, we must be flexible and change our approach based on the challenges and opportunities in front of us.

One way to understand the situationality of the development and utilization of the levels of complexity is through the types of questions we try to answer in and across contexts. Daniel Willingham (2009) reminds us that we should think of to-be-learned material as answers to core questions. Our work as teachers is to take the time necessary to explain to students the questions. Each level of complexity is primarily aligned to answering specific questions related to a learning goal (see figure 5.1). For instance, surface-level to-be-learned knowledge and skills are typically the answers to fact-based *what* questions and procedural *how* questions. Deep-level knowledge and skills are typically associated with answers to *why* questions. And, of course, transfer-level knowledge and skills are tied to questions that invite us to apply what we've learned across different situations.

Surface	Deep	Transfer
Who . . . ?	Why . . . ?	Should . . . ?
What . . . ?		When . . . ?
How . . . ?		Where . . . ?
		To what extent . . . ?

Figure 5.1: Surface, deep, and transfer inquiry prompts.

In the introduction, I defined *rigor* as the equal intensity and integration of surface-, deep-, and transfer-level learning. The integration of these levels of learning is critical for students to be successful both in and out of school. Over time, students must have the flexibility and fluidity to go back and forth along the continuum of surface, deep, and transfer learning to address a variety of questions. To begin this process of combining all levels of complexity, students typically start with developing an understanding of knowledge and skills in one of the areas of learning and over time begin to integrate that material with the other levels of complexity (see figure 5.2). The first level of understanding is one of isolation—comprehension within one of the key areas of learning. For instance, a student may understand that climate change affects animals and wish to create a proposal for her local community to mitigate these challenges. She sees broad connections between governmental policies and environmental science but lacks the surface- or deep-level knowledge in both disciplines.

However, as the student attends class, she starts to connect her transfer-level thinking to facts about greenhouse gases, the greenhouse effect, and policy development. At this point, she is linking her surface- and transfer-level knowledge and skills; these are level 2 connections. Over time, she develops a deeper understanding of the underlying principles of environmental science, government, and economics. Eventually, she takes action by running for student council and lobbying the school board to pursue renewable resources for her school. This is level 3, where she presents an integrated approach to all levels of complexity, illustrating the responsibilities that she, the school board, and the community have with regard to global warming. She demonstrates a level of cognitive flexibility, or agility, in moving back and forth across surface, deep, and transfer knowledge and skills.

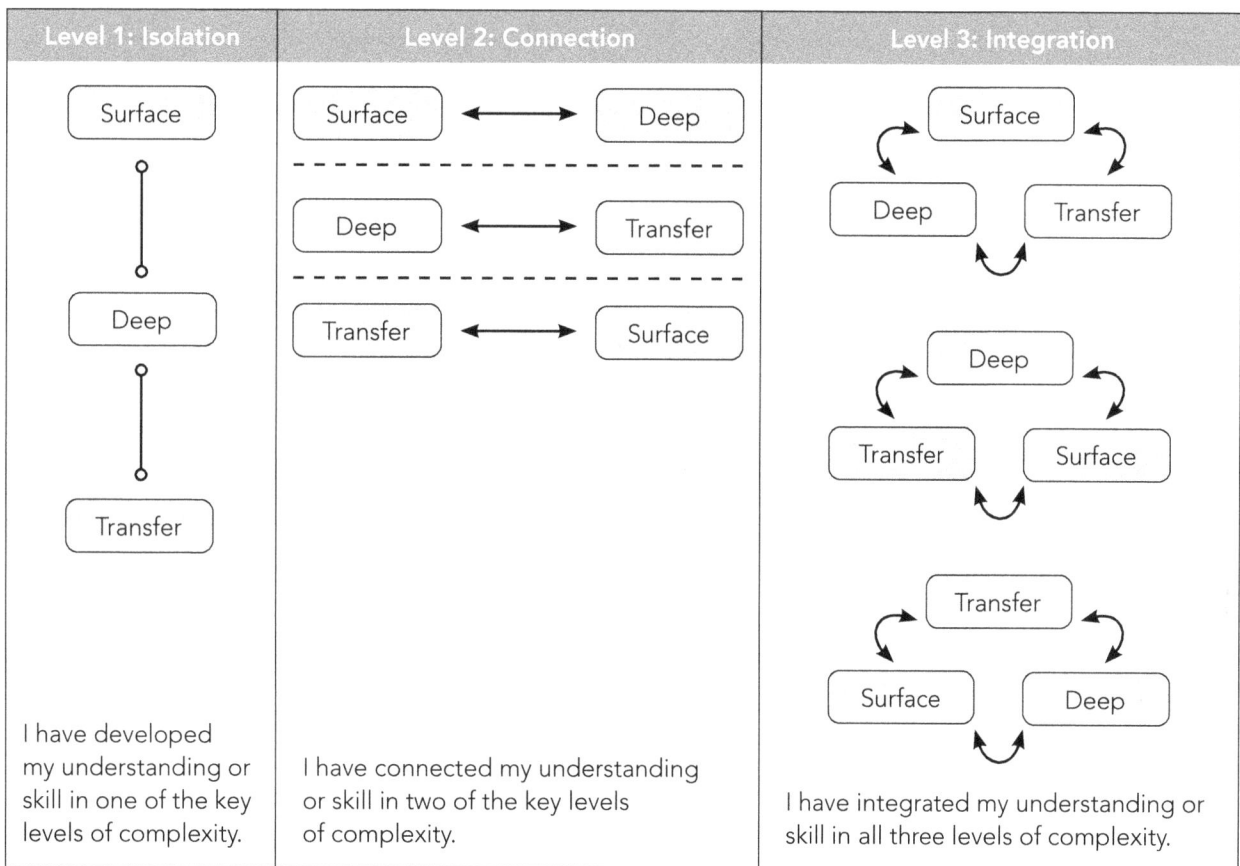

Figure 5.2: Levels of surface, deep, and transfer learning.

One of the greatest challenges of being a teacher is supporting every student in the classroom in meeting surface-, deep-, and transfer-level expectations. Figure 5.3 (page 100) illustrates the types of experiences that students may encounter in the classroom related to their level of understanding at any given time.

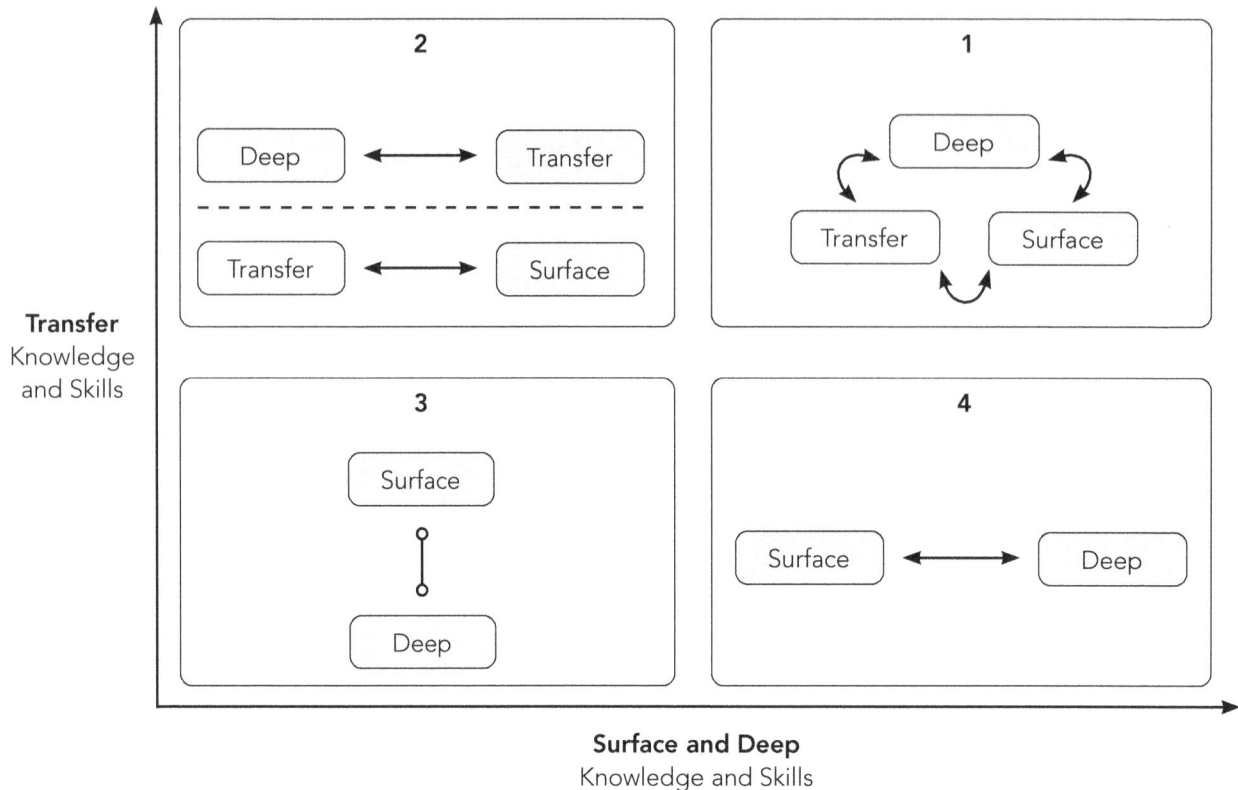

Figure 5.3: Matrix for the integration of all levels of complexity.

Given the four quadrants in figure 5.3, students may face at least four different types of experiences in the classroom, based on their level of knowledge at surface, deep, and transfer levels of complexity. Table 5.1 provides a description of the role teachers play in each of these situations.

To assist students in fully integrating surface, deep, and transfer knowledge and skills over time, follow these steps.

1. Prioritize the core curriculum standards.

2. Select a pathway for students to learn all three levels of complexity.

3. Ensure assessment practices integrate all levels of complexity.

4. Work collaboratively to inspect your impact and invent innovative units of study.

Prioritize the Core Curriculum Standards

Given the typical timetables teachers have for covering standards, along with the normal constraints of a class schedule, teachers simply can't always have students engaging in quadrant 1. Professionals don't always engage in that level of work either. Students need balance, and finding opportunities for students to enter into, say,

Table 5.1: Quadrant Descriptions

Quadrant	Teacher Roles and Responsibilities
1. Integrating Surface, Deep, and Transfer Students will apply core content knowledge and skills within and across disciplines and leverage efficacy-based strategies to solve problems within and across disciplines and contexts.	• Utilize strategies to develop students' ability to engage in activation, application, and authenticity at the transfer level. • Introduce a series of changes in perspective, and infuse perplexity in the learning process. • Integrate learning intentions and success criteria at surface and deep levels of learning with transfer success criteria. • Instruct and assess student performance toward transfer-level success criteria. • Co-construct success criteria with students, using multiple examples of success across multiple contexts. • Create lessons that align instruction, feedback, and learning strategies to levels of complexity. • Incorporate efficacy-based strategies into classroom instruction.
2. Connecting Transfer Knowledge and Skills to Surface and Deep Knowledge and Skills Students will develop a set of skills at the transfer level and begin to find ways to use those skills in one or more disciplines.	• Teach the skills of transfer: activation, application, and authenticity. • Model for students how transfer-level success criteria relate to surface and deep knowledge.
3. Isolating Surface and Deep Learning Students will develop knowledge and skills at one level of complexity in one discipline.	• Provide instruction, feedback, and learning strategies at either surface- or deep-level learning. • Incorporate efficacy-based strategies to support students at one level of complexity. • Integrate learning intentions and success criteria at the surface or deep level of complexity. • Instruct and assess student performance at one level of complexity.
4. Connecting Surface and Deep Knowledge and Skills Students will connect surface- and deep-level knowledge within a discipline.	• Create lessons that align instruction, feedback, and learning strategies to surface and deep levels of knowledge and skills. • Incorporate efficacy-based strategies into classroom instruction. • Integrate learning intentions and success criteria at surface and deep levels of complexity.

quadrant 4 is more important than figuring out how they can do quadrant 1–level work all the time. Moreover, not all curriculum standards within a discipline require the full integration of surface, deep, and transfer learning. The demands of certain standards require an intentional focus at all levels of complexity, whereas others require a cursory level of knowledge. According to authors Tammy Heflebower, Jan K. Hoegh, and Philip B. Warrick (2014), one way to begin this process is to evaluate your current standards and identify those standards that meet the following five criteria.

1. **Endurance:** Knowledge and skills that will last beyond a class period or course

2. **Leverage:** Knowledge and skills that cross over into many domains of learning

3. **Readiness:** Knowledge and skills important to subsequent content or courses

4. **Teacher judgment:** Knowledge of the content area and the ability to identify more- and less-important content

5. **Assessment:** Students' opportunity to learn content that will be assessed

Standards that meet these criteria are those teachers should use to ensure students integrate all three levels of complexity.

One note of caution when going through this process is that you must have a substantial number of declarative-knowledge outcomes that you are prioritizing for students. *Declarative knowledge* refers to informational knowledge such as facts, principles, concepts, and vocabulary. An example of declarative knowledge is a student's understanding place value in mathematics. Conversely, *procedural knowledge* is knowledge related to skills and strategies such as rules and tactics (Marzano, 2009). Knowing that you "carry the one" when adding three-digit numbers is procedural knowledge.

A challenge we have seen in the research is that educators often overvalue skills and deemphasize core content knowledge. As Willingham (2009) states, "Factual knowledge must precede skill" (p. 19). This simply means that without core knowledge, students are unable to utilize key skills, such as those associated with critical thinking—analyzing and synthesizing information. It is hard to think critically about something when you don't know anything about it. One suggested approach to easing into this process is to highlight core declarative-knowledge standards that meet the aforementioned criteria for all levels of complexity. Then teachers can spend time building units of study that ensure students experience surface, deep, and transfer learning. Next, teachers can go back and identify key procedural-knowledge standards that are necessary at all levels of complexity.

Once teachers identify key learning outcomes for students, teachers should plan how they want to *sequence* the levels of complexity for students.

Select a Pathway for Students to Learn All Three Levels of Complexity

Interestingly, there are multiple pathways teachers can take with students to meet surface-, deep-, and transfer-level expectations. In this book, I'll present three possible sequences. When you review them, please remember two things: (1) all levels of complexity are of equal value, and (2) the level of intensity for each level of complexity is dependent on students' prior knowledge.

Surface, deep, and transfer learning are not necessarily sequential. As we have gathered from previous chapters, a teacher could start students with an entry event and present a transfer-level problem on day 1 of a unit. For example, a teacher could show kindergarten students a slightly stretched-out Slinky, and he might place a base-ten block next to it for comparison purposes. He could then ask the students, "How do we begin to measure the length of the Slinky?" This would move the class into surface and deep instruction. He would then teach the basics of counting (that is, surface and deep learning). Finally, students would go back to the Slinky problem and attempt to solve it, discuss estimates, and potentially engage in a sequel to the problem: "How long is the snake in this picture?" This is a problem-based pathway because it begins with a transfer-level problem or challenge up front—rather than, say, instruction on counting (surface learning).

Figure 5.4 illustrates the three suggested pathways for integrating the levels of complexity. The pathways have been divided into the following three phases.

1. **Phase 1: Entry point**—The level of complexity at which students begin the sequence of learning

2. **Phase 2: Connection**—The level of complexity at which students work to relate knowledge and skills at two levels of complexity

3. **Phase 3: Integration**—The level of complexity at which students work to solve transfer-level problems that integrate surface and deep knowledge and skills

With a *traditional pathway*, a student's entry point is at the surface level of complexity, and then the student proceeds to deep and transfer learning over time (see figure 5.5, page 105). In this pathway, students typically initiate the learning sequence by answering *what* and *how* questions. Over time, students address questions at the deep and transfer levels of complexity. A *conceptual pathway* starts students at the deep level of learning and then guides them toward surface and transfer learning (see figure 5.6, page 105). Finally, the *problem-based pathway* starts students at the transfer level of complexity and leads them to the deep and surface levels (see figure 5.7, page 106). It is important to note that figures 5.5–5.7 display rather linear pathways but that in reality the sequence is much more fluid, as students may need additional support at other levels at different times in the learning sequence.

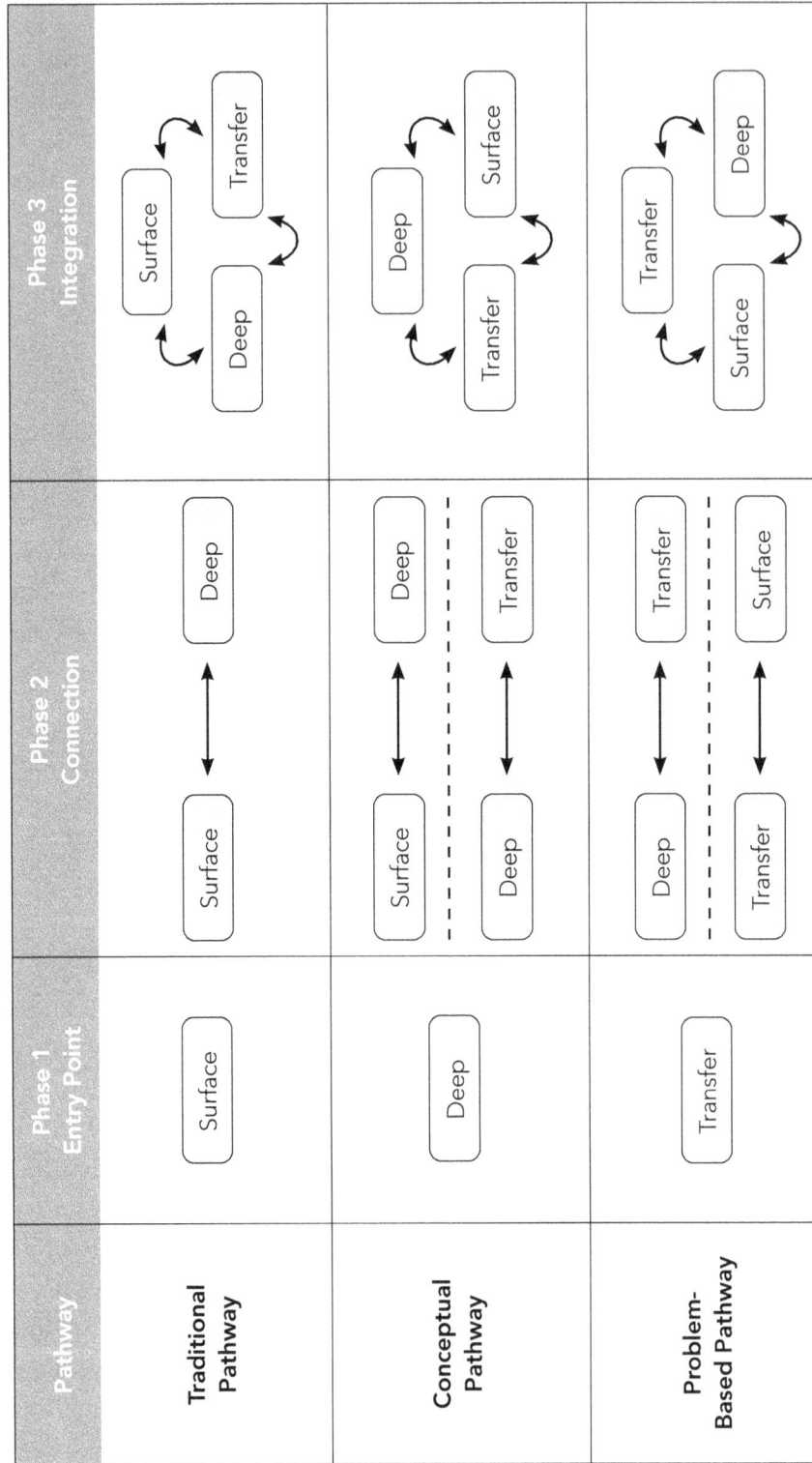

Pathway	Phase 1 Entry Point	Phase 2 Connection	Phase 3 Integration
Traditional Pathway	Surface	Surface ↔ Deep	Surface ↔ Deep ↔ Transfer
Conceptual Pathway	Deep	Surface ↔ Deep ¦ Deep ↔ Transfer	Deep ↔ Transfer ↔ Surface
Problem-Based Pathway	Transfer	Deep ↔ Transfer ¦ Transfer ↔ Surface	Transfer ↔ Surface ↔ Deep

Figure 5.4: Visual framing of levels of complexity.

SURFACE

SURFACE

TRANSFER

DEEP

DEEP

SURFACE

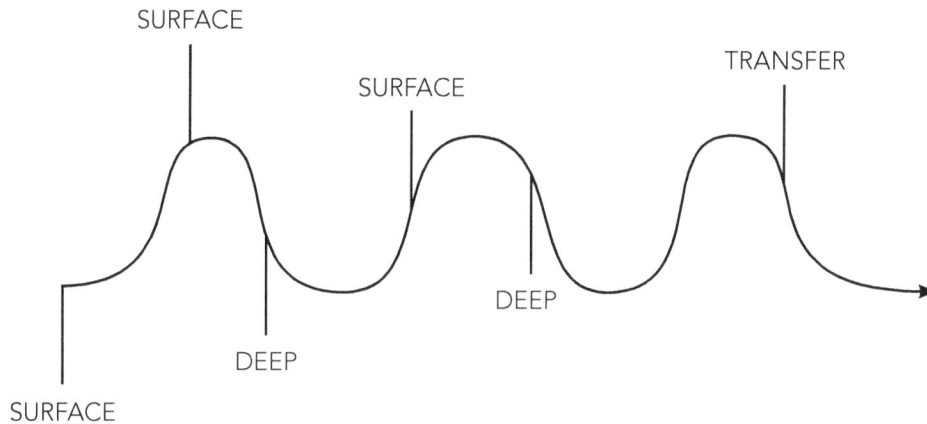

Figure 5.5: Traditional pathway.

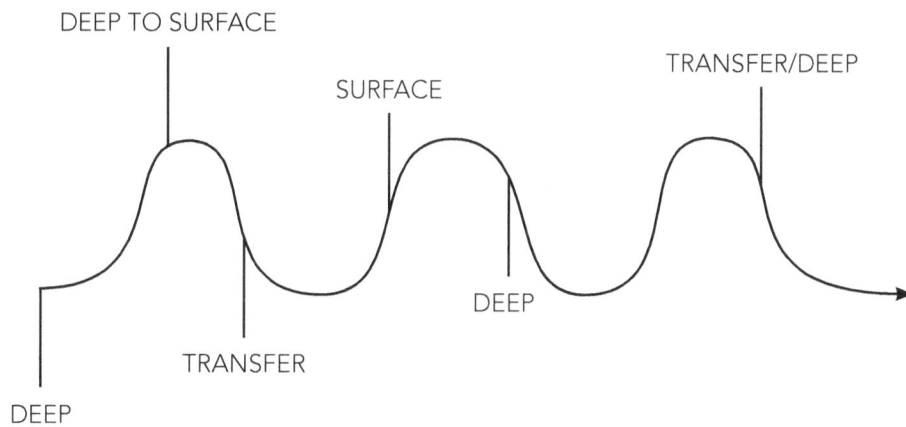

DEEP TO SURFACE

SURFACE

TRANSFER/DEEP

TRANSFER

DEEP

DEEP

Figure 5.6: Conceptual pathway.

The conceptual pathway begins with students evaluating the purpose, relationships, and principles of a particular discipline. The learning sequence begins at deep learning and then goes toward surface and transfer learning, not necessarily in that order. Typically, the questions students are solving at the conceptual level are *why* based—for example, *Why did Picasso create* Guernica?

A problem-based pathway begins at the transfer level. Students are presented with a challenging question that is typically asking *when* and *where* a set of concepts, skills, and general principles apply within and across contexts. Over the course of the unit, students learn the surface- and deep-level knowledge necessary to answer the transfer-level questions.

A teacher must strongly evaluate a problem-based pathway before introducing such a unit to students because problem- and project-based learning (PBL) have a checkered past, often yielding a low effect on student learning (Hattie, 2009). The method wasn't designed for surface learning, though when we look at the method's

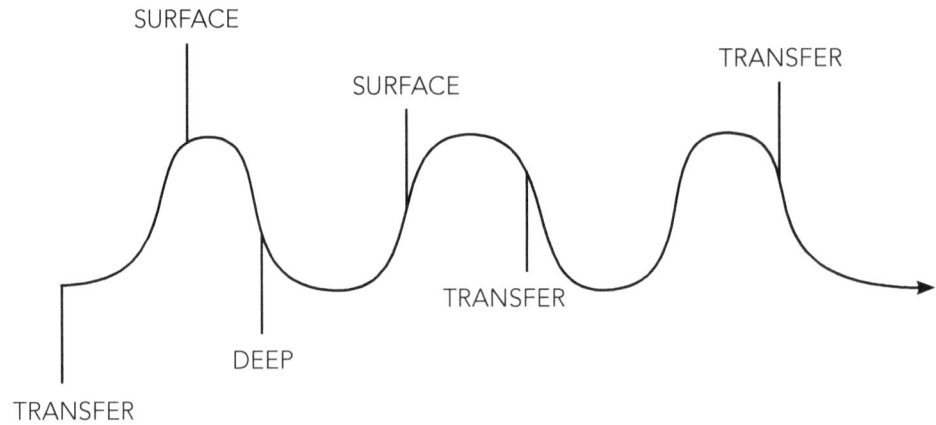

Figure 5.7: Problem-based pathway.

impact at deep and transfer levels, the effect on student learning is much higher (McDowell, 2017, 2018). When teachers incorporate high-yield instructional practices (for example, direct instruction) at the surface level with the high-impact practices of PBL (for example, comparing contexts), the gains at all levels of complexity are ideal (McDowell, 2017).

One suggested strategy that may be helpful in selecting a pathway is using the question-stem approach. As stated earlier in this chapter, surface, deep, and transfer success criteria may be viewed as answers to key questions. When deciding the best pathway for students, consider identifying the best sequence for students to sustain a level of inquiry across surface, deep, and transfer levels of complexity. To start this process, convert success criteria into a series of questions, and then choose the pathway that will allow students to answer those questions over time. Figure 5.8 illustrates a set of success criteria at each level of complexity that are then transformed into questions (derived from the stems in figure 5.1 [page 98]).

Learning Intention: I will apply multiplication of fractions.		
Surface-Level Success Criteria	**Deep-Level Success Criteria**	**Transfer-Level Success Criteria**
Multiply fractions. Define *multiplication of fractions*.	Justify and estimate the products of two fractions.	Apply multiplication of fractions in different contexts.
Surface-Level Questions	**Deep-Level Questions**	**Transfer-Level Questions**
How do I multiply fractions? What is the *multiplication of fractions*?	Why do we multiply fractions? Why are my solutions to problems correct or close to being correct?	When would the multiplication of fractions be helpful in real-world situations?

Figure 5.8: Success criteria and corresponding questions.

Using questions often enables teachers to picture the most appropriate and engaging sequence for students to learn and integrate surface, deep, and transfer knowledge and skills. Most important, teachers can use these questions when initiating instruction with students. Building an entry point around a question positions students as active participants in their learning. The question indicates a need for students to engage in their own learning and implies that teachers are not going to simply bestow knowledge. Once teachers have chosen the entry point, they may sustain students' use of questions by following one of the three pathways. In other words, teachers sustain student inquiry through a unit of instruction by selecting a pathway and then using questions as a guide for students to navigate the pathway of surface, deep, and transfer levels of complexity.

Let's look at a few near-transfer examples of converting content expectations to questions across levels of complexity. These examples span across elementary school (figure 5.9 and figure 5.10), middle school (figure 5.11, page 108), and high school (figure 5.12, page 108).

Learning Intention: I will compose an opinion on a topic. (CCSS.ELA-Literacy.W.K.1)

Surface	Deep	Transfer
• Identifies a topic • Lists opinions on a topic • Identifies an opinion	• Provides rationale for an opinion • Compares other opinions to a self-selected opinion	• Applies an opinion to other contexts

Key Questions

Traditional pathway: What are the key elements of creating an opinion in writing?

Conceptual pathway: Why should we consider the author's opinion?

Problem-based pathway: Where can we most effectively persuade others to agree with our position?

Source for standard: NGA & CCSSO, 2010a.

Figure 5.9: Elementary English language arts example.

Figure 5.10 shows sample questions aligned with traditional (surface), conceptual (deep), and problem-based (transfer) pathways. These questions are related to elementary-based mathematics outcomes.

Traditional pathway: What is addition? How do we add?

Conceptual pathway: Why does adding two quantities in different ways always provide the same sum?

Problem-based pathway: To what extent is addition limiting to our ability to understand the world?

Figure 5.10: Elementary mathematics example.

Figure 5.11 shows sample questions aligned with traditional (surface), conceptual (deep), and problem-based (transfer) pathways. These questions are related to middle school English language arts standards.

> Traditional pathway: How do we find the theme of a text? How is the theme conveyed? What is the theme?
>
> Conceptual pathway: Why do we see recurring themes in literature?
>
> Problem-based pathway: Who deserves forgiveness?

Figure 5.11: Middle school English language arts example.

Figure 5.12 shows sample questions aligned with traditional (surface), conceptual (deep), and problem-based (transfer) pathways. These questions are related to high school art, English language arts, and social studies standards.

> Traditional pathway: What aspects of art are conveyed in this piece? How does art convey recurring themes?
>
> Conceptual pathway: Why do humans continue to convey the human condition in works of art?
>
> Problem-based pathway: Where can we influence future generations in making better decisions?

Figure 5.12: High school art, English language arts, and social studies example.

Ensure Assessment Practices Integrate All Levels of Complexity

Once you have established pathways, you must incorporate assessment practices that allow you, as well as students, to confirm students have successfully integrated all levels of complexity.

McTighe and Wiggins (2013) argue for the use of open-ended assessment tasks at transfer-level learning. While a closed-ended question can typically be answered with a *yes* or *no* response or has a limited set of possible answers (for example, A, B, C, or D in a multiple-choice test), an open-ended question requires students to generate a response in which they explain their rationale, evaluate perspectives, and solve real-world problems (for example, an essay or problem-solving task). Open-ended assessments give students a way to illustrate the integration of surface, deep, and transfer learning. Moreover, open-ended assessments allow teachers to see whether students are using transfer skills—activation, application, and authenticity—in their work.

Figure 5.13 offers three types of open-ended assessments that students may engage in at the transfer level.

Transfer Assessment Type	Description	Examples
Products	Have two key phases—a proposal stage (identify a need, create criteria for solutions, and identify a solution) and a marketing-and-maintenance stage (pitch, create, market, and inspect; Zhao, 2012).	• Develop a movie. • Write a script. • Create a business plan. • Generalize core principles from case-based studies. • Formulate future proposals, solutions, and potential problems from case-based studies. • Design reports and present on problems to a panel of experts. • Create artwork, diagrams, charts, and graphs illustrating underlying patterns between different concepts and between different contexts.
Performances	Require students to apply knowledge and skills to solve complex problems across various contexts.	• Perform an act. • Debate. • Participate in a Socratic seminar. • Put on a talk show. • Conduct a science experiment. • Select a presentation strategy for offering a solution to a driving question (for example, a podcast or slide deck).
Portfolios	Ask students to compile a collection of artifacts that illustrate levels of learning over time. Such long-term perspectives provide a gauge of students' own learning or progress throughout their tackling of transfer-level problems.	• Produce journal entries or reflective writing on growth. • Conduct peer reviews of each other's progress and proficiency in developing levels of efficacy. • Present to a guest panel of community members on individual growth in meeting surface, deep, and transfer expectations. • Design a website that illustrates growth of learning, including evidence of work over time (for example, audio recordings and sample work with feedback).

Figure 5.13: Types of open-ended assessment tasks.

One of the most powerful aspects of open-ended tasks is that they are well suited for students' interaction with one another. When student interaction is leveraged, students have the opportunity to test prior knowledge and generate new ideas by:

▸ Giving one another feedback

▸ Engaging in problem solving

> ▸ Focusing on individual and collective understanding
> ▸ Encouraging participation of those with divergent viewpoints
> ▸ Allowing for different means of conveying understanding (for example, reading, writing, and debate)

Products, performances, and portfolios allow for conversations between peers and move away from tasks that simply reinforce prior knowledge or require little to no interaction between students. The conversations students have don't simply reinforce what they already know but rather venture into what they don't know or what is not fully formed in their minds; they unlock ways to integrate surface, deep, and transfer learning. This is where great learning occurs.

One approach teachers may take to engage students in open-ended tasks is to include a number of products, performances, and portfolios throughout a selected pathway. For example, students may design a podcast, collect data on their own performance to include in a portfolio, and then lead a question-and-answer session in front of a panel of experts.

Let's look at an example. Perhaps students are presented with the driving question, When and where should shelter-in-place orders be lifted during the COVID-19 pandemic? Here, the teacher may task students with developing a script for a podcast. In this podcast, students share with listeners their initial answer to the driving question. Furthermore, they may also collect data on closed assessment tasks (for example, in microbiology, the multiple-choice question, What is a virus?), as well as feedback from the podcast to include in their portfolio.

At this point, the teacher may invite students to use protocols to give one another feedback and share key ideas related to surface, deep, and transfer knowledge. As shown throughout this book, protocols are powerful ways to structure student interaction, and they also serve as a way for teachers to witness student thinking and intervene when necessary. Following this step, students receive new information on federal and state responses to the pandemic, as well as testing data on the spread of the disease. They then engage in performance activities in which they must communicate to a panel of news reporters their perspective on what nations should do in light of the data.

Work Collaboratively to Inspect Your Impact and Invent Innovative Units of Study

Robert J. Marzano, Philip B. Warrick, Cameron L. Rains, and Richard DuFour (2018) and John Hattie (2015) suggest effective collaboration with colleagues is one of the best strategies teachers can utilize to impact student learning. Teams enable teachers to listen to and share diverse viewpoints, engage in ample dialogue, and engage in collective decision making.

The purposes of teacher collaboration include:

- Making evidence-informed decisions in the areas of efficacy (orientation, activation, and collaboration) and expertise (surface, deep, and transfer)

- Developing transfer-level units of instruction

- Collecting data on students' ability to apply their learning, engage with others, and handle setbacks and ambiguity—in other words, their proficiency with transfer

If there is one core strategy that is both a blessing and a curse in work life and education, it is the use of teams. Filled with potential, teams often miss the mark on meeting objectives that require deep- to transfer-level work. Countless books have been written on the matter (Argyris & Schön, 1996; Schwarz, 2013, 2017). Most teams resort to a divide-and-conquer strategy: members divvy up tasks, separate from one another, and complete surface tasks with maximum efficiency. But like gardens, teams need tending. To develop and maintain strong teams, teachers should make use of the following.

- **Pact:** An agreement on how to work together and how to solve problems

- **Problem solving:** A process by which teammates identify a problem, agree on steps for solving the problem, and use a set of protocols to solve the problem

- **Perspective:** The use of ideas from others to build relationships, create shared understanding across diverse perspectives, and solve problems

Figure 5.14 (page 112) details specific strategies that student and teacher teams may use to ensure an effective and efficient impact on learning at expertise and efficacy.

Pact

Teams need a covenant, a pact for what people agree to compromise on in order to achieve through a collaborative experience. Psychologist and consultant Roger Schwarz (2017) provides a powerful model for teams to consider when they are looking at shared values and assumptions. He argues that people—and groups or teams of people—can often act one way and think they are acting another way. He uses the term *theories in use* to describe what we actually do and *espoused theories* to describe what we say we do. Schwarz (2017) maintains that espoused theories and theories in use should be aligned and centered on a *mutual-learning* approach, as opposed to a *take-control* or *give-up-control* approach. Perhaps the best way to understand whether our espoused theories and theories in use are aligned is to watch our own behavior when we encounter situations that are psychologically threatening or potentially embarrassing. A pact enables us to clarify the theories in use teams expect, what

Teaming Success Criteria	Description	Strategies
Pact	Teams identify commitments they will make to ensure all members work together to solve key problems for the team.	• Mutual learning, values and assumptions, and commitment • Agreements • Protocols
Problem Solving	Teams identify the type of problem they are solving and utilize a specific process and set of protocols to solve the problem.	• Type 1 inquiry cycles • Type 2 inquiry cycles
Perspective	Teams establish a specific structure to ensure that multiple perspectives are incorporated in understanding and solving problems.	• Priming • Protocols • Process roles

Figure 5.14: Teaming success criteria.

actual behaviors or theories in use specifically look like, and what teams may do if a member does not meet the specifications outlined in the pact.

Table 5.2 illustrates different theories of action based on values and assumptions leaders hold about power and influence. When teams have not spent time determining how to share power and influence, individuals may scramble to take control over the situation or work to give up all control to other members of a team. As we can see in table 5.2, the assumptions, strategies, and outcomes of these approaches inhibit learning. Teams must intentionally establish how they will mutually learn together by discussing the values, assumptions, strategies, and outcomes of mutual learning. Teacher teams should review this table and discuss steps their members could take to ensure that the teams stay in the area of mutual learning.

Table 5.2: Values, Assumptions, Strategies, and Outcomes Models

	Take Control	Give Up Control	Mutual Learning
Values	• Winning • Being right • Minimizing expressions of negative feelings • Acting rational	• Everyone participating in defining the purpose • Everyone winning and no one losing • Expressing one's feelings • Suppressing using one's intellectual reasoning	• Valid information • Free and informed choice • Intrateam commitment • Compassion

Assumptions	• I understand the situation; those who disagree don't. • I am right; those who disagree are wrong. • My motives are pure; those who disagree have questionable motives. • My feelings and behaviors are justified. • I am not contributing to the problem.	• I understand the situation; those who disagree don't. • I am right; those who disagree are wrong. • My motives are pure; those who disagree have questionable motives. • My feelings and behaviors are justified. • I am not contributing to the problem.	• I have some information; others have other information. • Each of us may see things the others do not. • Differences are opportunities for learning. • People are trying to act with integrity given their situations.
Strategies	• Advocating for my position • Keeping my reasoning private • Not asking others about their reasoning • Easing in • Saving face	• Advocating for my position • Keeping my reasoning private • Not asking others about their reasoning • Easing in • Saving face	• Testing assumptions and inferences • Sharing all relevant information • Using specific examples and agreeing on what important words mean • Explaining reasoning and intent • Focusing on interests, not positions • Combining advocacy and inquiry • Jointly designing the approach • Discussing undiscussables • Using a decision-making rule that generates the commitment needed
Outcomes	• Misunderstanding, unproductive conflict, and defensiveness • Mistrust • Self-fulfilling, self-sealing processes • Limited learning • Reduced effectiveness • Reduced quality of work life	• Misunderstanding, unproductive conflict, and defensiveness • Mistrust • Self-fulfilling, self-sealing processes • Limited learning • Reduced effectiveness • Reduced quality of work life	• Increased understanding, more-productive conflict, and reduced defensiveness • Increased trust • Reduced self-fulfilling, self-sealing processes • Increased effectiveness • Increased quality of work life

Source: Adapted from Schwarz, 2017.

In order to operate in a mutual-learning approach, a pact should incorporate the strategies in the Mutual Learning column in table 5.2. Then teacher teams should select protocols that will enable members to engage in conversations, give and receive feedback, and solve problems. Protocols are structured ways to organize conversations around the key outcomes of the discussion while maintaining professional integrity and navigating emotions productively. Table 5.3 illustrates a number of protocols people may use to ensure effective feedback and gain perspective from others. See figures A.5 (page 132) and A.6 (page 133) in appendix A for more information on the critical-friends protocol and the learning-dilemma protocol, respectively.

Table 5.3: Feedback Protocols

Protocol	Description
Critical Friends	Feedback should be affirmative, offer key questions for the recipient to consider, and provide concrete next steps to enhance performance.
Tuning	Feedback should be affirmative and offer key questions for the recipient to consider. This is similar to the critical-friends process except that it does not provide next steps. Visit the School Reform Initiative website (www.schoolreforminitiative.org), choosing Protocols from the Protocols and Resources drop-down menu, for a detailed outline on how best to conduct this protocol developed by Joseph McDonald and refined by David Allen (2017).
Learning Dilemma	Feedback occurs in cases where team members are just starting to develop or execute a solution to a problem and need further input in order to proceed.
Consultancy	Feedback occurs when team members are in the middle of a project and need further input. Visit the School Reform Initiative website (www.schoolreforminitiative.org), choosing Protocols from the Protocols and Resources drop-down menu, for a detailed outline on how best to conduct this protocol developed by Faith Dunne, Paula Evans, and Gene Thompson-Grove (2017).

Problem Solving

Teacher teams should work to inspect student growth and proficiency toward efficacy-based knowledge and skills alongside the development and integration of surface-, deep-, and transfer-level knowledge and skills. Moreover, once teams inspect student performance, it is incumbent on teams to respond to such data. One way to do this is to follow these four steps.

1. **Diagnosis:** Team members meet and collect data to answer the question, To what extent are our students progressing toward efficacy and expertise? Once teachers collect initial evidence, they identify an area of focus for the team.

2. **Intervention:** The team identifies and implements intervention strategies that members believe will make a substantial impact on student learning.

3. **Analysis and evaluation:** Team members meet and review the results of their intervention on student performance. During this time, the

team determines next steps to either maintain current practices or adjust its strategies.

4. **Learning:** Team members take time together to reflect on key learning during the problem-solving process. This is a time for the team to determine the effectiveness of specific instructional strategies on student learning.

These steps repeat themselves over and over, forming cycles. The Ross School District engages in these cycles every four to five weeks (see figure 5.15, page 116, for an example of growth data). Teachers in this district typically select a tool to measure student growth and proficiency in the area of student expertise or efficacy (see table 5.4, page 117) and then collect diagnostic data. After the diagnostic data are reviewed, teachers determine an area of focus, establish a goal, and select a solution that they think will work for making an impact on student learning. Then the team members come back together every week or so to determine successes, challenges, and next steps. Team members determine their overall impact and whether they should maintain the interventions they have put into place or they should adjust or remove a specific practice. Finally, teams reflect on their key learning from the experience and devise potential next steps for the team. At Ross School District, approximately 70 percent of all collaborative time is spent engaging in these cycles of diagnosis, intervention, analysis and evaluation, and learning.

Teachers need ample time and feedback from colleagues to design and inspect the impact of their transfer-level work with students. The following three steps will support teams as they find ways to incorporate transfer learning into the classroom and inspect student growth toward transfer learning.

1. **Explore:** Teachers need time to design units of study that include transfer-level learning. Often, this means teachers are working with their colleagues to find ways to connect learning outcomes and contexts within and across different academic disciplines. In addition, this means that teachers are looking to find multiple ways for students to express their understanding of transfer-level learning. For example, teachers in different departments may meet and share learning intentions and surface and deep success criteria they will be expecting students to meet in the next quarter. Next, the teachers work together to create transfer-level success criteria that require students to use the knowledge and skills in each class to solve a real-world problem or problems in one or more contexts (see table 2.1, page 43).

2. **Engage:** Teachers need to work with colleagues to find experts outside of school who are working on real-world problems, involved in the community, and willing to support teachers and students in transfer-level work. This is also the time to discuss the most effective open-ended tasks for the transfer-level unit of study.

Metric		Pretest Avg.	Posttest Avg.	Difference
Correct	# Correct	6.8	12.4	5.6
	% Correct	42.8%	77.3%	34.5%
	# + Transfer		13.5	6.6
	% + Transfer		84.2%	41.4%
Passing	# Passing	5	13	8
	% Passing	26.3%	68.4%	42.1%
	# + Transfer		13	8
	% + Transfer		68.4%	42.1%
Score Standard Deviation (STDEV)		4.7	2.8	−40.8%

* A lower STDEV indicates students are performing more similarly.

* Index is how well they did compared to the average score.

Module 1: Multiplication and Division

Total available points:	16		16							
	Pretest	% Correct	Posttest	% Correct	Transfer	Posttest + Transfer	% Correct + Transfer	Growth	Pretest Index	Posttest Index
Student 1	1	6.3%	12	75.0%	1	13	81.3%	11	0.15	0.97
Student 2	4	25.0%	14	87.5%	0	14	87.5%	10	0.58	1.13
Student 3	2	12.5%	12	75.0%	0.5	12.5	78.1%	10	0.29	0.97
Student 4	8	50.0%	8	50.0%	0	8	50.0%	0	1.17	0.65
Student 5	6	37.5%	10	62.5%	0	10	62.5%	4	0.88	0.81
Student 6	8	50.0%	16	100.0%	2	18	112.5%	8	1.17	1.29
Student 7	4	25.0%	9	56.3%	0	9	56.3%	5	0.58	0.73
Student 8	3	18.8%	8	50.0%	1.5	9.5	59.4%	5	0.44	0.65
Student 9	2	12.5%	12	75.0%	0	12	75.0%	10	0.29	0.97
Student 10	13	81.3%	12	75.0%	2.5	14.5	90.6%	−1	1.90	0.97
Student 11	16	100%	16	100.0%	3	19	118.8%	0	2.34	1.29
Student 12	3	18.8%	10	62.5%	0	10	62.5%	7	0.44	0.81
Student 13	13	81.3%	16	100.0%	1	17	106.3%	3	1.90	1.29
Student 14	14	87.5%	16	100.0%	3	19	118.8%	2	2.05	1.29
Student 15	2	12.5%	14	87.5%	1	15	93.8%	12	0.29	1.13
Student 16	12	75.0%	16	100.0%	2	18	112.5%	4	1.75	1.29
Student 17	5	31.3%	10	62.5%	0	10	62.5%	5	0.73	0.81
Student 18	7	43.8%	12	75.0%	1.5	13.5	84.4%	5	1.02	0.97
Student 19	7	43.8%	12	75.0%	2	14	87.5%	5	1.02	0.97

Source: © *2019 by Ross School District, Ross, California. Used with permission.*

Figure 5.15: Example of assessment data illustrating growth over time at all levels of complexity.

Table 5.4: Expertise- and Efficacy-Based Tools

Developing Expertise	Developing Efficacy
Effect size—Using pre- and postassessment data, teachers analyze proficiency and progress set against the .40 effect size. (Hattie, 2012)	Learning rounds—Teachers have students take short interviews and participate in focus groups about their understanding, use, and perception of efficacy-based knowledge and skills. Teachers collect these data throughout the school year. (McDowell, 2018)
Knowledge gain—Establishing a set scale for levels of complexity, teachers analyze the amount of growth for students in their learning. (Marzano & Waters, 2009)	Survey data—Teachers have students take surveys related to efficacy-based knowledge and skills before and after a lesson, a unit of study, or challenging transfer-level assessment tasks. (McDowell, 2018)
Standardized benchmarking—Teachers use a standardized assessment throughout the year to track student growth.	Focus groups—Teachers interview a few students to get a sense of their progress and proficiency related to efficacious behaviors.
Work-sample evaluations—Teachers evaluate student work over time to identify growth in performance at all levels of complexity.	Interviews—Teachers meet with students one-on-one to gain an in-depth understanding of students' perceptions of the value and use of efficacious behaviors.
Interviews—Using similar questions to those posed on pre- and postassessments, teachers interview students one-on-one. These interviews often use clarifying questions to get an in-depth understanding of expertise. (Marzano, 2009)	Unobtrusive assessments—Through observations during class, teachers identify the frequency of efficacy-based behaviors.
Unobtrusive assessments—Through observations before, during, and after class, teachers mark down changes in the use of efficacious behaviors in the classroom. (Marzano, 2009)	Student-generated assessments—Teachers empower students to create their own approaches to demonstrating their progress and proficiency over time. (Marzano, 2009)
Discussion—Using prompts at surface, deep, and transfer levels, teachers can track student progress toward outcomes.	Discussion—Using prompts at orientation, activation, and collaboration levels, teachers can track student progress toward outcomes.

Source: Adapted from McDowell, 2019.

3. **Evolve:** Teachers need feedback from colleagues on how to continually augment their transfer-level work to ensure relevance in and across different professions. They may do so by inspecting the impact of their transfer-level work with students and making use of data to improve transfer-level opportunities for students.

Table 5.3 (page 114) illustrates recommended protocols for supporting teacher teams in learning how to teach for transfer, while table 5.5 (page 118) illustrates protocols for teachers to invent, implement, and inspect transfer-level work. The tools cited in the following table are described in figure 4.8 (page 92).

Table 5.5: Inspecting and Improving Transfer-Level Instruction

Element	Description	Tools
Explore	Teachers develop transfer-level units of learning for students and leverage feedback from colleagues to refine initial ideas for transfer.	• Skunk Works
Engage	Teachers work with others outside the school and other departments to develop transfer-level work.	• Search paths for shared interests
Evolve	Teachers seek feedback to improve their work over time.	• Future forecasts • Red team

Perspective

The World Bank invests in a multitude of projects in developing countries to support education, health care, infrastructure, and resource management. One of the most interesting findings from the World Bank is that the most successful projects are those that have been inundated with conflicts and crises. In fact, Hirschman (as cited in Gladwell, 2013) claims that instead of asking what benefits a project has yielded, it would be almost as pertinent to ask, "How many conflicts has it brought in its wake?" and "How many crises has it occasioned and passed through?"

One of the most important skills a student can learn—and a teacher can model—is how to appreciate and respect doubt in one's own thinking and approach to a problem. We often see doubt as a deficit; we associate doubting one's ideas with negative self-talk. But it doesn't need to be. We need to see doubt as an asset to our learning. Doubt is having the strength or courage to believe in yourself while also being open to questioning your ideas. This is hard but fruitful work.

Doubt allows us to step back from our stances, our perspectives, and our realities and look beyond our noses. Doubt doesn't mean we disengage or dismiss information. Rather, doubt is about our having the strength to suspend or hold our ideas while we explore something new. Like lifting a car's hood to see the engine, doubt allows us to look at the internal workings of our ideas and beliefs. As historian Jeremy Adelman (as cited in Gladwell, 2013) writes of philosopher Eugenio Colorni, "Colorni believed that doubt was creative because it allowed for alternative ways to see the world, and seeing alternatives could steer people out of intractable circles and self-feeding despondency. Doubt, in fact, could motivate."

Doubt doesn't mean that we don't advocate for our ideas; it means that we advocate for our ideas *and* use questions to seek out others' ideas and perspectives. Doubt is the fertile ground of inquiry and a key ingredient to the mutual-learning approach discussed earlier. We should speak like we are right and listen like we are wrong. How, then, do we embrace and use the power of doubt? I recommend teachers use the approaches detailed in figure 5.16—priming, protocols, and process roles—to engage in conversations that enable members of collaborative groups to listen to one another and solve problems.

Approach	Description	Example
Priming	Teachers use protocols to elicit assumptions, biases, and perspectives from other teachers.	• A list of questions is provided to teachers to reflect on their own perspectives and those of others—for example, Whose voices are we not actively listening to? What would be other ways to interpret the data? Who else should we talk with? What would be another solution that would meet our criteria?
Protocols	Teachers use structured processes for problem solving and decision making.	• Critical-friends protocol • Tuning protocol • Learning-dilemma protocol • Consultancy protocol
Process Roles	Members of teacher teams take on individual roles to ensure that the core strategies of the mutual-learning model are active in the group at all times.	• Perspective coach: A person designated to make sure different perspectives are heard • Accuracy coach: A person designated to ensure that information used in solutions is conveyed accurately • Agreement coach: A person designated to ensure that members adhere to agreements with the mutual-learning approach during meetings

Figure 5.16: Mutual-learning approaches.

Conclusion

Teachers must strategically plan for and establish strategies for ensuring students integrate efficacy- and innovative expertise-based knowledge and skills. In this chapter, I've proposed key strategies for moving toward such aims, including prioritizing the core curriculum standards, selecting pathways for students to learn all three levels of complexity, ensuring assessment practices that integrate all levels of complexity, inspecting our impact on student progress and proficiency, and designing innovative units of study.

Reflection Questions

The following questions are designed for you to address individually or in teams to determine the next steps that you will take in the classroom. When you review these questions, it is important that you reflect on the tools you currently use with students and where you may discover tension between your current beliefs and practices and what I've proposed. Educators usually carry with them a set of tools that work well in certain situations. This chapter's contents may have been somewhat familiar to those teachers who have tools that work well in the garage. Teachers who come with a set of tools suited to the office, however, may have found this chapter challenging. Regardless of where you stand, this is an opportunity for you to incorporate new tools.

1. What were your major takeaways from this chapter?

2. Which question stems presented in figure 5.1 (page 98) do you often expect students to answer? Why?

3. Which of the four strategies proposed to integrate surface, deep, and transfer knowledge and skills appears to be the most doable? Why? Which strategy appears to be the most difficult? Why?

4. What steps need to be taken to develop priority standards? What steps need to be taken to ensure that students are learning declarative knowledge across all subjects?

5. What pathway have you used to ensure students experience surface-, deep-, and transfer-level learning?

6. What open-ended assessment tasks are you unfamiliar with? What would you need to do to try a new form of assessment?

7. What steps would you need to take to support you and your team in inspecting your impact on student learning and innovating new units of study?

Next Steps

As with the reflection questions, please go through each of these steps individually or as a team and determine what actions you will take in your classroom.

1. Review this chapter with colleagues, and discuss changes you can make to help your team work toward meeting surface-, deep-, and transfer-level expectations. Ask the following questions.

    a. How does our team currently work to inspect impact, invent new units, and improve work? How are these processes similar to or different from what is discussed here?

    b. What actions would we need to take to follow the three steps (that is, explore, engage, and evolve) to invent and inspect transfer-level work with colleagues?

2. Select a previous chapter with your colleagues, and discuss the similarities and differences between the chapter's recommendations and

your and your colleagues' current teaching practices. Discuss as a team why such similarities and differences exist and what next steps the team should take. Two strategies that may assist in this discussion include:

a. Engaging in a final-word protocol (see table 5.6)

b. Jigsawing the chapter you chose (Visit EL Education [n.d.; https:// eleducation.org] for a detailed outline on how to carry out the jigsaw protocol.)

Table 5.6: Final-Word Protocol

Purpose

The following protocol ensures teams have a collective understanding of research, student work, or other written material.

Suggested Time

Forty-five minutes

Opening Moves (Introduction) (five minutes)

- Review purpose of protocol.
- Review agreements, or norms, of the team.
- Identify facilitator and participants.
- Review success criteria of product, process, or presentation being evaluated.

Procedure

Step 1: Preparation

Participants read a designated piece before entering the protocol.

Step 2: Starting a Round (seven to ten minutes)

- Participants form groups of four to five and designate someone to start the process.
- The selected person reads a quote or makes a comment that stands out regarding the piece of writing. This person does not elaborate (thirty to forty-five seconds).
- Each participant then has sixty seconds to respond to the quote or comment. No one else speaks. Once one person is finished, the next person responds until everyone has had a chance to speak.
- The first person shares the final word by summarizing what was heard and providing a comment of the person's own.

Step 3: Repeating the Round

The group then goes through the process until every participant has had a chance to provide an initial quote or comment and the final word.

Closing Moves (five minutes)

Participants rate how well the team executed the protocol and followed agreements.

EPILOGUE

And what does he do to make these great rock bands better? Well,
he makes a mess. He disrupts their creative processes. It's his role
to tell them that they have to play the unplayable piano.

—TIM HARFORD

Musician Brian Eno has been a collaborator on some of the most influential and successful rock and roll albums ever made. He takes a unique approach to assisting musicians in their creative processes. He interrupts their music making and tells them to change instruments, work at a different speed, or experiment with a mistake they've made in playing a song (Harford, 2015). When he does this, band members become frustrated because they have to stop relying on their routines and practices and instead attempt something new. Unable to use their familiar tools and stay in the predictable environment of the office, they begin to tinker. They look laterally, find the adjacent possible, and create—the work innovators take up in the garage.

The framework I have laid out in this book is essentially a how-to guide on Brian Eno's work with musicians—combining expertise with innovation—but in the field of education. We as teachers need to pause and set aside our routines and practices, looking to unfamiliar, perhaps uncomfortable approaches that will improve our students' capacities to acquire core content knowledge, build efficacy in their own learning, and develop the skills to solve real-world problems across multiple contexts. This is accomplished by first using our familiar tools in the office—teaching and assessing students' learning toward core learning outcomes, as well as co-constructing such intentions so that students gain a high level of clarity in what we expect of them and are able to support one another. Next, we pick up the tools we can find in the garage; we incorporate change in the learning experience, and we teach students how to look across problems, handle variability, engage with others outside the classroom, and solve perspective-laden problems. Finally, we must work together to create the conditions that will transform the classroom into a breezeway that integrates the work of the garage and the office.

As educators, we must actualize in the classroom the work laid out in this framework, ensuring students develop core academic knowledge and skills and the means to take ownership over their own learning. We must help them forge the tools they need to address real-world problems that require unique insights across contexts and solutions that incorporate multiple viewpoints. Let's not just imagine this environment; let's take action. We can do this not by throwing away all our tools but by keeping those that work, discarding those that don't produce the desired results, and picking up a few new ones to move all students forward toward transfer learning. If we do this, students will find balance in the space between the office and the garage and take control over not only their learning but their lives and futures. We have a great influence on this trajectory. This is, after all, what we are here for: to ensure students become what they are capable of becoming—people who can transfer the knowledge and skills in the classroom to their larger world.

AFTERWORD

by Tammy Heflebower

Michael McDowell built this tremendous learning model for teachers from the premise of providing students with clear expectations through significantly deeper learning. It is nothing short of brilliant. When McDowell mentions, "The key to transfer is comparison. People must look *across* rather than *within*—*wide* rather than *narrow*, *open* rather than *closed* . . . Transfer is at the heart of this book, but transfer cannot occur without educators who promote rigor" (p. 4), he captures the next steps with engaged and expanded learning.

Throughout my career spanning over three decades, I have learned much about how to design, use, and teach others about quality curriculum, instruction, and assessment practices. The foundation for my deeper understanding was initially captured through the awareness and use of *proficiency-level descriptors* (Guskey, 2009; Heflebower, 2005). These specific documents, which correspond to the most important student learning goals, clarify and extend explicit learning for students.

This work began in the late 1990s with a nudge from a keen mind and non-conformist commissioner of education in Nebraska, Doug Christensen, and his unconventional and highly competent assessment director, Pat Roschewski. They both collaborated with and challenged me to help create local assessment systems that would meet or exceed quality standards that kept students at the center. This transformative work and additional partnership with the Buros Center for Testing was the basis for my dissertation in 2005 and a metamorphosis that changed me as an educator. My continued collaboration with incredible colleagues—including Robert Marzano, Bev Clemens, Phil Warrick, Jan Hoegh, and Janelle Wills, to name a few—helped me in transferring my initial thinking and use of proficiency-level descriptors into what we have now defined and explicated as *proficiency scales*. They are progressions of learning that are the origin for sound instructional planning, quality feedback, students tracking their progress and setting goals, and high-quality classroom assessments (Guskey, 2009; Heflebower, 2005; Heflebower et al., 2014; Heflebower, Hoegh, Warrick, & Flygare, 2019; Marzano, 2010). They delineate content and skills derived from a set of prioritized learning standards ranging from simple (2.0) to target (3.0) to complex (4.0). I see McDowell's propositions explained in *Teaching for Transfer* as nothing short of a comparable monumental shift for *instructional* thinking and planning. His framework fits perfectly for capturing the expertise and efficacy these levels require, yet with instructional focus and rigor. His surface content and skills connect to what are denoted as the simple 2.0 content and skills, his deep instructional strategies mirroring more the target level (3.0) and further pushing teaching strategies into the transfer or complex (4.0) portion of a proficiency scale. All of these paired with the essential conative skills (Marzano & Heflebower, 2012) of student efficacy are the foundation for impacting student learning. Students' abilities to act on what they learn, deal with setbacks, use intrapersonal and interpersonal skills, and face life's never-ending challenges take the learning from merely something to master to the depths of true transformation and application.

McDowell's metaphor of the office and the garage in the introduction provides the imagery and application for enhanced learning. Too often, due to the mere nature of time constraints (180 days) driving learning, instead of learning driving time, students stay in the *office* and rarely experiment with the application of learning in the *garage*. What McDowell professes for the needs of students to transfer learning, he himself has emulated in creating this learning framework. He magnifies the needs for surface and deep knowledge, problem solving, contextual knowledge, and application. Simply put—surface and deep knowledge paired with transfer is the key to rigor. McDowell's further delineation of near transfer, near-to-far transfer, and far transfer adds more specificity to applying essential knowledge and skills. This collision of ideas across various contexts unlocks the unknown potential of each student. He puts forth the idea to *tinker* with what we already know, yet to wonder and test ideas in seemingly unrelated contexts, while pairing all this with both perspective and perplexity. His suggestion of this stretch—while taking problem-based learning across various disciplines—is splendid.

What I may appreciate most is McDowell's keen ability to explain the instructional construct and provide a myriad of practical strategies and applications. I am especially intrigued by the co-construction of expectations not only with students but also with those outside the schooling environment. This is something that I believe in wholeheartedly and implemented during my most effective learning moments as a classroom teacher—long before McDowell's marvelous construct and applicable verbiage. I especially appreciate his skillfulness in taking that beyond students' applying such learning to truly transform the world as they know it. His analogous comparison in the introduction with those firefighters who were unable to reconstruct and problem solve during tragic fires was the difference between life and death. This is the same way our students may maintain low-level surface learning without the means to tackle life's immense and imminent challenges. It is the difference between staying at levels 2 and 3 on a proficiency scale and pushing more students into the deeper level 4 territory. The challenge is in ensuring the depth of understanding and connectivity among the disciplines in order to construct learning experiences to exemplify such overarching connections.

McDowell urges us all to lean into those practices that challenge our thinking. These may greatly expand our inventiveness and impact learners to survive those new challenges that we cannot even yet imagine. His expansive resources form such a foundation of transfer. He epitomizes the idea of educational knowledge and theories blended with other disciplines, like sociology, biology, digital media, the performing arts, and so on, and he tracks these connections throughout. As he states, "finding spare parts from different fields and applying them to new problems" (p. 20) is not only what he challenges us to do with students but what he himself models. We need our learners today to be the leaders of tomorrow—employing the transfer of surface and deep learning for purpose and function across disciplines. What McDowell outlines is taking that progression of learning and understanding into unforeseen territories. McDowell's work will help you reimagine classrooms and will be referenced for years to come.

APPENDIX A: RESOURCES FOR FOUNDATIONAL LEARNING

Learning Intentions and Leveled Success Criteria Across Grade Levels

The following two figures provide examples of learning intentions and leveled success criteria, which will support you in the development of your own.

Learning Intention: I will generate and solve real-world problems using the first quadrant of the coordinate plane.		
Surface Content (Focuses on one concept or multiple concepts)	**Deep Content** (Connects concepts, ideas, and skills)	**Transfer Content** (Applies concepts, ideas, and skills)
Identify points graphed in the first quadrant of the coordinate plane. Graph points in the first quadrant of the coordinate plane. Identify coordinate values of points in context.	Interpret coordinate values of points in context. Explain the meaning of coordinate values of points in context.	Create real-world problems that can be solved by graphing in the first quadrant of the coordinate plane.

Figure A.1: Learning intentions and leveled success criteria, grade 6 mathematics.

Learning Intention: I will evaluate solutions and nonsolutions for systems of equations in various contexts.		
Surface Content (Focuses on one concept or multiple concepts)	**Deep Content** (Connects concepts, ideas, and skills)	**Transfer Content** (Applies concepts, ideas, and skills)
Determine whether a point is a solution to a system given a graph or equation.	Interpret solutions in context where constraints are presented verbally. Represent constraints by equations and systems.	Defend and justify solutions in context.

Figure A.2: Learning intentions and leveled success criteria, grade 10 mathematics.

Strategies for Testing Prior Knowledge and Developing Efficacy

The following figure offers a number of strategies to enable teachers to instruct students on how to test their current knowledge and actively focus on improving their learning over time.

Strategy	Description	Activity
Discrepancy Analysis	This is a collaborative activity that enables students to see their gaps in learning and plan next steps.	• Ask students to take a preassessment. • Ask students to determine their level of confidence in their performance on the preassessment. • Hand back the preassessments with correct answers, and have students review the work with partners. • Students discuss with partners gaps in knowledge. • Student groups discuss potential next steps to reduce the gaps and share key ideas with the class.
Share, Test, and Verify	Students share with other students their prior knowledge, including misconceptions; determine ways to test future thinking to better engage with content; and then reflect with other students at the end of a lesson or unit.	• Ask students to write down what they know about a topic. • Instruct students to find a way they can test what they know to make sure they are right (for example, "How do we question what we know?"). • Students pair up and discuss their "knows" and steps to clarify any gaps in their learning. • Student groups share with the class and discuss ways to track progress. • Student groups come back at the end of the lesson or unit and discuss ideas that they originally had correct and others that have changed.

| Error-and-Correction Process | Teachers and students collaborate to build success criteria. The teacher models common mistakes and has students work to correct those mistakes, and then the class practices building criteria together by writing down how the teacher could have prevented the mistakes. This works best when students have some prior knowledge in the activity to draw on. | • State the learning intention to students.
• Tell students that you will model the work, and ask them to watch you to make sure you don't make any mistakes.
• Make an intentional mistake, and say, "Oh no, what have I done?"
• Once students articulate the mistake, ask the students what you could do to prevent the mistake from happening again.
• Record their ideas under the heading *Success Criteria*.
• Repeat the process through all success criteria.
• Ask students to pair up and monitor each other in the same task using the newly developed success criteria.
• Reflect on what mistakes students noticed and when they were unaware or didn't know how to articulate a mistake. This provides useful data regarding areas in which students may lack prior knowledge and need instructional support. |

Figure A.3: Testing-prior-knowledge activities.

The following figure illustrates sample strategies to support students in building their efficacy (orientation, activation, and collaboration) in learning over time.

Title	Description	Example
Orientation: **Mix and Match**	This activity enables students to identify the context, learning intention, work structure, and tasks connected with a learning goal.	Give students a set of cards, in which each card features an example of a context, learning intention, work structure, or task connected with a learning goal. Students work with others to identify which card is the context, learning intention, work structure, or task. Students then share their answers with others and discuss the correct answers.
Activation: **"When I'm Stuck"**	This activity puts students in challenging cognitive situations and requires them to reflect on the best possible strategies to address the challenge. These cognitive situations may include scenarios, problems, or games in which students must discuss what steps they would take to move through the challenge and how they would use those steps generally to be successful in other situations.	Place students into groups and ask them to solve one of four problems. During their discussions, stop the students and ask them what strategies they are using to find a solution to the problem. At the conclusion of the activity, student groups reflect on how their approach to problem solving could be used in their academic learning.

Figure A.4: Efficacy-based strategies.

continued →

| Collaboration: Digging Deeper | This activity requires students to form groups and present their individual understanding of a concept or context to one another and then discuss how their individual understanding is similar to and different from other students'. Next, students dialogue on steps they can take to check one another's ideas and come to an accurate consensus. Finally, the group reflects on the importance of bringing individual ideas and understanding to the group, as well as the importance of working together to ensure collective accuracy of information. | Have students form groups of three, and ask them to individually solve a problem presented on a small whiteboard or sheet of paper. Ask students to write down their background knowledge for the problem they are solving (for example, "What do you know that helps you answer this problem?"). Next, the students share their answers and background knowledge. Ask the student groups to discuss the similarities and differences between members' answers and background knowledge. |

Feedback Protocols

The following two figures describe two possible protocols you may use when working with colleagues to solve problems.

Critical-Friends Protocol	
Ten minutes	An individual (or team) presents a piece of professional work or student-performance data to elicit colleagues' feedback. This could be an example of learning intentions and success criteria, a unit of study, or perhaps pre- and postassessment data. The presenter shares for approximately seven to eight minutes. The last two to three minutes are designated for providing clarification in response to faculty members' questions.
Five minutes	The presenter prepares to record notes, and the faculty members serve as "critical friends," offering feedback in a structured manner. For the first two minutes, critical friends should highlight the strengths of the presenter's work, using statements that begin with "I like." For the remaining minutes, critical friends should pose questions for the presenter to consider, or make statements that begin with "I wonder." The presenter should not speak during this time but rather listen and record notes as colleagues provide feedback.
Five minutes	The presenter reflects on the comments and identifies probable next steps.

Figure A.5: Critical-friends protocol.

Purpose

This protocol enables presenters in teacher team meetings to think more expansively about a particular dilemma.

Process

Presenter provides an overview of the dilemma (five to ten minutes)

Group asks clarifying questions (three to five minutes)

Group asks probing questions of the presenter (ten minutes)

Group analyzes the dilemma, refining the issue and then providing open suggestions; presenter does not speak (ten minutes)

Presenter reflects on the presenter's thinking with the group (three to five minutes)

Facilitator reflects on the process with the group (three to five minutes)

Probing Questions

What did we hear?

What didn't we hear that might be relevant?

What assumptions seem to be operating?

What questions does the dilemma raise for us?

What do we think about the dilemma?

What might we do or try if faced with a similar dilemma?

What have we done in similar situations?

Figure A.6: Learning-dilemma protocol.

APPENDIX B:
RESOURCES FOR TRANSFER-NETWORK DEVELOPMENT

Success-Criteria Examples

The following figure offers examples of success criteria at the transfer level. The middle column provides transfer-level statements without any situation or context, while the right-hand column illustrates each statement with a contextualized example.

Success-Criteria Prompts Students:	Context-Specific Success-Criteria Examples Students:
• Formulate a proposal	• Formulate a proposal to enhance the global economy without the use of unilateral tariffs
• Generalize the solution to situation X to situation Y	• Generalize the solution of reducing pesticides in farming to the reduction of carbon dioxide in the ozone
• Design and conduct an investigation	• Design and conduct an investigation on the favorability of Medicare coverage for all people in nearby counties
• Hypothesize the outcome of _____ if we engage in _____	• Hypothesize the outcome of increasing exercise if we incorporate a financial incentive
• Initiate the following solution with _____	• Initiate the use of restorative practice with young (five- to seven-year-old) children who fail to meet school expectations
• Reflect on the implementation of _____	• Reflect on the implementation of the use of drones to ticket speeding cars
• Research _____	• Research new technologies related to learning and determine the need for changing current policy

Figure B.1: Transfer-level success-criteria examples.

The following figure offers examples of learning intentions, success criteria, contexts, and driving questions for interdisciplinary transfer-level units of study.

Disciplines	Learning Intentions	Success Criteria	Contexts	Driving Questions
Environmental Studies **English Language Arts** **Social Studies**	Students will: • Conduct short or sustained research projects • Analyze the major social problems and domestic policy issues in contemporary American society (HSS.11.11) • Consider the global impact of local and regional activities and evaluate and propose solutions to a variety of issues, including ozone depletion, global warming, ocean warming and acidification, invasive species, and human impacts on diversity	Students will: • Answer a question (including a self-generated question) or solve a problem; narrow or broaden the inquiry when appropriate; and synthesize multiple sources on the subject, demonstrating understanding of the subject under investigation (W.11–12.7) • Gather relevant information from multiple authoritative print and digital sources, using advanced searches effectively; assess the usefulness of each source in answering the research question; and integrate information into the text selectively to maintain the flow of ideas, avoiding plagiarism and following a standard format for citation (W.11–12.8) • Trace the impact of, need for, and controversies associated with environmental conservation, expansion of the national park system, and the development of environmental protection laws, with particular attention to the interaction between environmental protection advocates and property rights advocates (HSS.11.11.5)	• Shipping-lane speed limits • *Moby Dick*	• In what ways can we change the adversarial relationships that humans have with some animals? • To what extent should humans take responsibility for spaces such as oceans and outer space that are not owned by any species?

	Students will:	Students will:	• *The Story of Glass* • *1984*	• To what extent can we ensure that the future prospects of all people are positively impacted by current and past technological innovations?
English Language Arts **Chemistry**	• Know that the periodic table displays the elements in increasing atomic number and shows how periodicity of the physical and chemical properties of the elements relates to atomic structure (HS-PS1-1) • Provide a complex analysis of two or more central ideas of a text (RI.11–12.2)	• Relate the position of an element in the periodic table to its atomic number and atomic mass • Use the periodic table to identify metals, semimetals, nonmetals, and halogens (HS-PS1-1) • Cite strong and thorough textual evidence to support analysis of what the text says explicitly, as well as inferences drawn from the text, including determining where the text leaves matters uncertain (RI.11–12.1) • Determine two or more central ideas of a text and analyze their development over the course of the text, including how they interact and build on one another to provide a complex analysis; provide an objective summary of the text (RI.11–12.2) • Analyze a complex set of ideas or sequence of events and explain how specific individuals, ideas, or events interact and develop over the course of the text (RI.11–12.3)		

continued →

Figure B.2: Learning intentions and success criteria for interdisciplinary driving questions.

Disciplines	Learning Intentions	Success Criteria	Contexts	Driving Questions
Biology **English Language Arts**	Students will: • Apply the idea that biological evolution accounts for the diversity of species developed through gradual processes over many generations (HS-LS4) • Write informative or explanatory texts to examine and convey complex ideas, concepts, and information clearly and accurately through the effective selection, organization, and analysis of content (W.9–10.2)	Students will: • Describe how both genetic variation and environmental factors are causes of evolution and diversity of organisms (LS4.C) • Clarify the reasoning used by Charles Darwin in reaching his conclusion that natural selection is the mechanism of evolution (HS-LS4–4) • Analyze how independent lines of evidence from geology, the fossil record, and comparative anatomy provide the bases for the theory of evolution (HS-LS4–1) • Construct a simple branching diagram to classify living groups of organisms by shared derived characteristics and determine how to expand the diagram to include fossil organisms (LS4.A) • Recognize that extinction of a species occurs when the environment changes and the adaptive characteristics of a species are insufficient for its survival (LS4.C)	• On the Origin of Species • Star Wars • Social programs	• To what extent can humans control evolution in its many forms? • Should humans manipulate evolutionary processes?

- Introduce a topic; organize complex ideas, concepts, and information to make important connections and distinctions; and include formatting (for example, headings), graphics (for example, figures and tables), and multimedia when useful to aiding comprehension (W.9–10.2.A)

- Develop the topic with well-chosen, relevant, and sufficient facts, extended definitions, concrete details, quotations, or other information and examples appropriate to the audience's knowledge of the topic (W.9–10.2.B)

- Use appropriate and varied transitions to link the major sections of the text, create cohesion, and clarify the relationships among complex ideas and concepts (W.9–10.2.C)

- Use precise language and discipline-specific vocabulary to manage the complexity of the topic (W.9–10.2.D)

- Establish and maintain a formal style and objective tone while attending to the norms and conventions of the discipline (W.9–10.1.D)

- Provide a concluding statement or section that follows from and supports the information or explanation presented (W.9–10.1.E)

Source for standard: Adapted from California Department of Education, 2000; NGA & CCSSO, 2010a; NGSS Lead States, 2013.

Near-, Near-to-Far-, and Far-Transfer-Unit Examples

The following three figures illustrate units of learning created by teachers to ensure students meet surface-, deep-, and transfer-learning outcomes.

Learning Intention
Students will analyze the development of federal civil rights and voting rights.

Success Criteria	
Surface	**Deep**
• Explain how demands of African Americans stimulated the movement for civil rights. • Examine the roles of civil rights advocates (for example, A. Philip Randolph, Martin Luther King Jr., Malcolm X, Thurgood Marshall, James Farmer, and Rosa Parks), including the significance of Martin Luther King Jr.'s "Letter From Birmingham Jail" and "I Have a Dream" speech.	• Examine and analyze the key events, policies, and court cases in the evolution of civil rights, including *Dred Scott v. Sandford*, *Plessy v. Ferguson*, *Brown v. Board of Education*, *Regents of the University of California v. Bakke*, and California Proposition 209. • Discuss the diffusion of the civil rights movement of African Americans from the churches of the rural South and the urban North, including the resistance to racial desegregation in Little Rock and Birmingham, and how the advances influenced the agendas, strategies, and effectiveness of the quests of American Indians, Asian Americans, and Hispanic Americans for civil rights and equal opportunities. • Analyze the passage and effects of civil rights and voting rights legislation (for example, the Civil Rights Act of 1964 and the Voting Rights Act of 1965) and the Twenty-Fourth Amendment, with an emphasis on equality of access to education and to the political process.

Contexts
• Dreamers under different presidential administrations • The reading wars (phonics versus whole-language instruction) • Redistricting

Transfer Success Criteria
• Hypothesize the changes to civil rights of Americans in the future. • Initiate an investigation with people who represent different demographics on federal civil rights and voting rights. • Research changes to federal civil rights and voting rights in the past ten years.

Driving Questions
• To what extent should federal civil rights and voting rights change in the future? • Should one branch of government have more power to lead changes to civil and voting rights in the future?

Tasks
• Present a proposal to a group of citizens and elected officials on changes that should be made to federal civil rights and voting rights and what actions they can take to make this work possible.
Perplexity and Perspective
• Consider the race- and class-based power dynamics between different groups of Americans in the northern regions of the country, and compare them to those of the southern regions (for example, review the bus-desegregation approaches of the North versus the South). • Introduce a new federal or state policy that offers additional funding in schools.

Figure B.3: Single within-discipline learning intention (near transfer).

Learning Intention		Learning Intention	
Students understand the major events preceding the founding of the nation and relate the significance of those events to the development of American constitutional democracy.		Students apply strategies that enable them to accurately and consistently interpret history.	
Success Criteria		**Success Criteria**	
Surface	**Deep**	**Surface**	**Deep**
• Describe the Great Awakening. • Identify the core elements of the Declaration of Independence that pertain to securing individual rights. • Construct a timeline of the American Revolution. • Identify the key countries involved and their role in the American Revolution. • Define civic republicanism, classical liberal principles, and English parliamentary traditions.	• Compare and contrast the moral and political ideas of the Great Awakening and the development of revolutionary fervor. • Analyze the philosophy of government expressed in the Declaration of Independence, with an emphasis on government as a means of securing individual rights. • Analyze how the American Revolution affected other nations, especially France. • Compare and contrast the nation's blend of civic republicanism, classical liberal principles, and English parliamentary traditions.	• Label different interpretations of history as *thematic*, *sequential*, *correlational*, and *causal*. • Identify the roles of chance, oversight, and error in history. • Determine the sources of historical data used to interpret past events. • Provide an example of how interpretations of history are subject to change as new information is uncovered.	• Explain the central issues and problems from the past, placing people and events in a matrix of time and place. • Distinguish cause, effect, sequence, and correlation in historical events, including the long- and short-term. • Connect multiple sources of historical ideas and events to explain the emergence of new patterns. • Evaluate sources of information and multiple interpretations of historical information to explain different viewpoints of historical events.

Figure B.4: Two within-discipline learning intentions (near-to-far transfer). continued →

Contexts
• Examine the real motives for the Boston Tea Party.
• Predict individual freedoms today (for example, the Second Amendment).

Transfer Success Criteria
• Formulate a prediction on how individual freedoms today were shaped by the formation of the Declaration of Independence.

Driving Questions
• Who secured individual rights through the forming of the United States, and who was left out?
• To what extent has the power of those initially left out changed over time?

Tasks

• Conduct a perspective analysis composed of five steps. The five steps, with corresponding questions, are recommended to provide a structure students can follow to develop and fortify their understanding of the content.
 	
  1. Identify your position on a controversial topic—What do I believe about this?
 	
  2. Determine the reasoning behind your position—Why do I believe that?
 	
  3. Identify an opposing position—What is another way of looking at this?
 	
  4. Describe the reasoning behind the opposing position—Why might someone else hold a different opinion?
 	
  5. Summarize what you have learned—What have I learned?

Perplexity and Perspective
• Perspective of African Americans in the American South, British royalty, and Native Americans
• Current: Hong Kong

Learning Intention

Students demonstrate basic economic reasoning skills and an understanding of the economy.

Success Criteria

Surface	Deep
• Identify the ways in which local producers have used and are using natural resources, human resources, and capital resources to produce goods and services in the past and the present. (HSS.3.5.1) • Explain that some goods are made locally, some elsewhere in the United States, and some abroad. (HSS.3.5.2) • Identify examples of the individual economic choices that involve trade-offs and the evaluation of benefits and costs. (HSS.3.5.3)	• Compare and contrast the ways in which local producers have used and are using natural resources, human resources, and capital resources to produce goods and services in the past and the present. (HSS.3.5.1) • Compare and contrast domestic and international trading. • Discuss the relationship of students' work in school and their personal human capital.

Learning Intention

Students generate measurement data by measuring lengths using rulers marked with halves and fourths of an inch.

Success Criteria

Surface	Deep
• Show the data by making a line plot, where the horizontal scale is marked off in appropriate units—whole numbers, halves, or quarters.	• Relate the horizontal scale to units of measurement.

Learning Intention

Students write informative or explanatory texts to examine a topic and convey ideas and information clearly.

Success Criteria

Surface	Deep
• Introduce a topic, and group related information together; include illustrations when useful to aiding comprehension. • Develop the topic with facts, definitions, and details. • Provide a concluding statement or section.	• Use linking words and phrases (for example, also, another, and, more, and but) to connect ideas within categories of information. • Relate the thesis to the conclusion.

continued →

Figure B.5: Multiple across-discipline learning intentions (far transfer).

Contexts

- Global trading (G7 policy decisions)
- Oil or gas
- Renewable energy
- School store
- Amazon rain forest

Transfer Success Criteria

- Formulate a position on whether there should be an external referee in making economic choices.
- Design and conduct a proposal for enhancing economic benefits for oneself or others.

Driving Questions

- Who is negatively impacted by the economy, and who is positively impacted?
- Should an external source influence our economic decisions? If so, to what extent?

Tasks

- Write an informational piece on how economics impacts third graders today and when they are older.

Perplexity and Perspective

- Introduce groups of people who are not part of a typical market economy.
- Introduce changes in supply chains, and discuss the impact such changes would have on the economy.

Source for standard: California Department of Education, 2000.

APPENDIX C:
RESOURCES FOR ENGAGEMENT
IN TRANSFER-LEVEL WORK

Transfer-Level-Learning Strategies for Students and Teachers

The following five figures illustrate suggested strategies and example techniques for enabling students to engage in transfer-level tasks.

Strategy	Description	Example
Flowchart (or Other Visual Representation)	Students use strategies that enable them to understand, represent, and show the correct procedure for a task or problem, the means for processing information related to a problem, and the various perspectives related to a problem.	• Claim-pass: A student writes down a claim on a sheet of paper and passes the paper to another student. This student records a piece of evidence to back up or reject the claim and passes the paper to another student, who must record a different piece of evidence to support or reject the claim. The students involved in the activity meet and reflect on and discuss what they could do to ensure that they have presented accurate evidence regarding the claim.
Protocols to Prime Transfer-Level Analysis and Problem Solving	Students use structured routines to problem solve—that is, identify problems, create criteria for success, develop potential solutions, select solutions, and implement solutions.	• SWOT (problem identification): Students chart strengths, weaknesses, opportunities, and threats to identify the problem. • Nice-toos, wants, needs (criteria selection): Students create a three-column chart to prioritize what is needed, desired, and optional for a solution. • Augmented brainstorm (potential solution identification): Students brainstorm ideas with occasional breaks to determine ideas that they want to continue to explore. • Critical friends (implementation): Students run a feedback protocol to determine progress toward goals and feedback on next steps.
Engagement Processes With Role Models, Experiences From Others, and Resources in Problem Contexts	Students use specific strategies for collecting and making sense of information from others.	• Three stay, one stray: Students form groups of four and complete a task. Each group then assigns one group member to visit another group and present the group's current solution. The new group's members then give feedback on the visiting group member's work and determine what changes they may make to their own work. The visiting member returns to the original group and delivers the feedback. The group decides on next steps.

Figure C.1: Processing-information and planning-next-steps strategies.

Strategy	Description	Example
Structured Protocols for Feedback at the Beginning, Middle, and End of Transfer Level	Use a variety of routines to ensure students are receiving as well as giving to others accurate feedback throughout the learning process.	• Critical-friends protocol
In-the-Moment Feedback Strategies	Use a variety of techniques to ensure students are receiving as well as giving to others accurate feedback during student and group independent practice.	• Surface, deep, and transfer inquiry prompts (Students and teachers use the inquiry chart in figure 5.1 [page 98] to ask students questions.)
Peer-to-Peer Feedback on Process	Establish specific routines for students to discuss the process of working together and the efficacy and effectiveness of problem solving.	• Process check • Third option

Figure C.2: Feedback strategies.

Habit	Description	Example
Generate Answers	Students create multiple answers and inspect answers with other students.	Pose a question, and tell students to generate multiple answers to the problem. State that they should estimate possible answers and different ways to illustrate answers (for example, visual or written). Students may work alone or with others to discuss, debate, and determine the appropriate answer and then share and discuss as a class. Review the answers and engage with students on inspecting the accuracy of the solution and interpretation of the problem.
Self-Testing	In order to find out what students understand and what they are unclear on in their learning, students take nongraded tests prior to studying or learning new core content in a class.	Provide definitions and have students generate potential terms that correspond with those definitions.
Process-Feedback Tactics	Students engage in a metacognitive practice of determining their current goals and progress, how they handle setbacks, and how they'll ensure accuracy of feedback both to and from others.	Prompt the students with questions associated with orientation, activation, and collaboration.
Wait Time and Conversations	Students address a question without teacher assistance. They converse with other students on approximate answers.	Prompt students with a question, and ask them to write down their current thinking and then discuss with others.

Search and Rescue	Students receive feedback (on their work and that of others) on an assessment or a response to a question, and they must determine with others what next steps they need to take.	Review a group's work and offer several pieces of feedback on sticky notes. Tell the students that they must identify what piece of feedback goes to which paper. Listen in on the inspection.
Metaphors	Students find a metaphor that best represents their ideas.	Provide a series of examples of a key concept, and ask students to find other ways to represent the concept (for example, a metaphor, a story, or a graphic).

Figure C.3: Habits of practice for feedback.

Strategy	Description	Example
Individual Learning Plan	This strategy enables students to identify their goals for a lesson or unit, as well as the steps they will take to meet stated goals. This strategy also allows students to reflect on their use of orientation, activation, and collaboration strategies over time.	Students fill out a Google Form that tasks them with identifying their daily and weekly goals and what steps they will take to meet those goals, including orientation, activation, and collaboration strategies they'll use to support themselves along the way. At the end of the day or week, students reflect on their growth and proficiency toward their established goals. This process allows students to determine next steps to enhance their learning.
Asset Approaches	This strategy enables students to shift toward an active response-oriented approach by focusing on the areas of control, impact, breadth, and duration.	Students follow a process similar to the one outlined in figure A.6 (page 133)—that is, the learning dilemma. The learning-dilemma protocol is a collaborative approach that positions students as guides to support peers in their learning. When students run through the protocol, peers use table 4.1 (page 78) to focus on the proactive strategies that others used or could use to improve.
Leveraging Breadth	This strategy supports students in understanding internal and external factors related to a problem they are investigating.	Students conduct an environmental scan, looking at internal issues, trends, and patterns, and then evaluate external factors that may have an influence on the context they are studying. They use qualitative and quantitative data, leveraging as many perspectives as possible.
Connections Across Contexts, Communities, and Content	This strategy enables students to consistently reflect on their work toward transfer-level learning and consider how that learning connects across different contexts and perspectives. It also ensures transfer-level work is connected to core surface and deep knowledge.	To determine the effectiveness of transfer-level learning across contexts and content, students use the thinking-hats strategy (de Bono, 1999).

Figure C.4: Reflecting-and-connecting strategies.

Strategy	Description	Example
Sentence-Stem Analogies	Ask students to create sentence-stem analogies for abstract concepts or ideas.	Provide students with stems that enable them to practice using analogies (for example, "_____ is the same as _____").
Visual Analogies	Ask students to create alternative ways to express analogies visually.	
Metaphors	Ask students to compare subjects in the form of a metaphor.	Provide students with subjects such as *America*, *the walrus*, and *NASA's decision to launch the* Challenger. Next, give students a list of verbs (for example, *was*, *is*, *are*, and *were*). Finally, have students create comparisons.
Similes	Ask students to make a comparison between two subjects using *like* or *as*.	Provide students with subjects such as *America*, *the walrus*, and *NASA's decision to launch the* Challenger. Have students create comparisons using *like* or *as*.

Figure C.5: Strategies for heightening comparisons through analogies.

Grade-Level Transfer-Unit Examples

The following three figures illustrate units of learning at the elementary, middle, and high school levels to ensure students meet surface-, deep-, and transfer-learning outcomes.

Teaching-for-Transfer Unit of Learning	
Learning Intention	**Learning Intention**
Students will: • Write opinion pieces (W.2.1)	Students will: • Recall information from experiences or gather information from provided sources to answer a question (W.2.8)
Success Criteria	
Surface Students will: • Introduce the topic or book they are writing about • State an opinion • Supply reasons that support the opinion • Use linking words (for example, *because*, *and*, and *also*) to connect opinion and reasons • Provide a concluding statement or section (W.2.1)	**Surface** Students will: • Use sources that are regarded as experts on a topic • Quote sources • Cite sources in the text

Deep	Deep
Students will: • Provide opinions other than their own with reasons that support such opinions • Use contrasting connectives (for example, *on the other hand* and *however*) to compare one opinion with another • Provide a concluding statement that summarizes the reasons for one opinion over another	Students will: • Relate sources to the author's opinion and diverging opinions

Transfer Success Criteria

Students will:

• Apply credible sources to convince others of an opinion

• Connect opinion writing and sources to core content in other disciplines

Contexts	• Organic lunches • Electric vehicles • Screen time in schools and at home

Questions

Surface	Deep	Transfer (Driving Questions)
• How do we persuade others through writing? • What is the most effective way to convince others of an opinion via writing? • How do we prevent (or enhance) human bias to persuade others of our opinions? • How do we ensure that our opinions are backed by research? • How do we defend our opinions against the arguments of others?	• Why do our opinions matter? • Why do sources strengthen opinions?	• Should we provide balanced viewpoints when sharing an opinion? • Who is the most vulnerable to bias in hearing others' opinions? • When are opinion pieces dangerous?

Tasks

Surface	Deep	Transfer (Products, Performances, and Portfolios)
Students will: • Draft an opinion piece • Submit original sources • Give and receive feedback on opinion pieces	Students will: • Write multiple opinion pieces across multiple contexts • Provide feedback to others regarding their opinion pieces	Students will: • Present a solution to a problem that has a multitude of opinions

Figure C.6: Second-grade near-to-far transfer.

continued →

Incorporating Perspective and Perplexity	
Perspective	**Perplexity**
• Ask students to flip perspectives on an original opinion piece of writing.	• Incorporate a new source that provides information that counters the original source. • Incorporate additional (sequel) context for students to write about or present on.

Lessons		
Surface	**Deep**	**Transfer**
• Co-construct success criteria by reviewing multiple examples of opinion pieces across different contexts. • Outline an opinion piece. • Conduct a jigsaw.	• Compare and contrast valid sources. • Evaluate sources of contemporary pieces of writing. • Draft and edit written opinion pieces.	• Prepare for an oral presentation. • Discuss sequels and the commonalities of opinion pieces. • Discuss bias.

How will you launch transfer-level work with students? [Narrative]

Present students with a biased piece of writing on the critical need for students to wear school uniforms. Students then evaluate this opinion piece and discuss the criteria they use to evaluate effective opinion writing. Draft the criteria with the students and then have students evaluate multiple pieces of student work that cover a number of different contexts. Next, give each student a situation (on a flash card) to write about. Tell the students that these flash cards may be switched later on and that students may have to express their opinions on a new topic or write a counternarrative.

Source for standard: Adapted from NGA & CCSSO, 2010a.

Teaching-for-Transfer Unit of Learning			
Learning Intention	**Learning Intention**	**Learning Intention**	**Learning Intention**
Students will: • Explain the passing down of genetic information from parents to offspring	Students will: • Draw inferences about one or more populations of organisms using random and representative samples	Students will: • Write informative or explanatory texts to examine a topic and convey ideas, concepts, and information through the selection, organization, and analysis of relevant content (W.7.2)	Students will: • Analyze the interactions between individuals, events, and ideas in a text (RI.7.3)

Success Criteria			
Surface Students will: • Define the terms *gene, chromosome, proteins, mutations,* and *traits* • List several examples of variations that arise from reproduction of cells • Identify examples of beneficial, harmful, and neutral changes to the structure and function of a protein	**Surface** Students will: • Rationalize the validity of generalizations via sampling • Define random sampling and representative samples and support valid inferences (7.SP.A.1) • Use data from a random sample to draw inferences about a population with an unknown characteristic of interest (7.SP.A.2) • Generate multiple samples (or simulated samples) of the same size to gauge the variation in estimates or predictions (7.SP.A.2)	**Surface** Students will: • Introduce a topic or thesis statement clearly • Include headings, charts, and tables • Develop a topic with facts, definitions, concrete details, quotations, and other information and examples • Provide a concluding statement • Establish and maintain a formal style	**Surface** Students will: • Describe how advancements and achievements influence scientists • Describe how advancements and achievements influence politicians • Describe how advancements and achievements influence the general public
Deep Students will: • Show cause and effect between chromosomal mutations and changes in proteins • Infer potential changes in future generations due to mutations and the environment	**Deep** Students will: • Use random sampling and representative samples to support valid inferences • Assess the degree of visual overlap of two numerical data distributions with similar variabilities, measuring the difference between the centers by expressing it as a multiple of a measure of variability (7.SP.B.3)	**Deep** Students will: • Organize the text using appropriate transitions to create cohesion and clarify the relationships among ideas and concepts (W.7.2.C) • Relate supporting evidence to key topics using precise language and discipline-specific vocabulary (W.7.2.D)	**Deep** Students will: • Analyze how advancements and achievements influence society

Figure C.7: Seventh-grade far transfer.

continued →

Transfer Success Criteria

Students will:

- Critique current and future approaches to forecasting future outcomes (for example, genetic inheritance and variations)

- Hypothesize new approaches to effectively and efficiently forecasting future outcomes

Contexts	
	• Retroviruses
	• Cancer
	• Marfan syndrome
	• Sickle cell disease
	• Leber hereditary optic neuropathy
	• Codominant inheritance pattern
	• Fragile X
	• Hemophilia
	• Swyer syndrome
	• Down-Turner syndrome
	• Uniparental disomy (Prader-Willi syndrome)

Questions

Surface	Deep	Transfer (Driving Questions)
• What is a chromosome? • What does it mean to have a disorder? • How do you draw inferences? • What are the key components of a successful informational piece of writing? • How do we analyze the interactions between individuals, events, and ideas in a text? (RI.7.3)	• Why is citing evidence critical to writing informational pieces? • Why do mutations cause positive, neutral, and negative effects? • Why is sampling a critical tool for making assumptions about populations?	• Should we continue to invest in research to predict future conditions? • Where can we modify future outcomes?

Tasks

Surface	Deep	Transfer (Products, Performances, and Portfolios)
Students will: • Write an informational piece of writing • Read texts related to genetic mutations and inferential statistics • Complete mathematics assignments related to statistics and probability	Students will: • Debate the probabilities of mutations in future populations and the technology to reduce the impact of mutations • Give and receive feedback on writing, mathematics, and science tasks • Defend lab results	Students will: • Present to an audience on forecasting approaches • Produce an informational writing piece that supports the argument presented

Incorporating Perspective and Perplexity	
Perspective	**Perplexity**
• Present students with scenarios that may include governmental overreach, religious conflicts, and overall ethics of genetic testing to present a larger social context of genetics outside of biology.	• Change the specific genetic mutation students are evaluating, and have students compare and contrast the mutations. • Add the complications of reduced penetrance into students' discussions. • Have groups of students investigate chance processes and develop, use, and evaluate probability models standard to the mathematics work (7.SP.C.5). • Have groups of students apply measures of center and measures of variability for numerical data from random samples to draw informal comparative inferences about two populations (7.SP.B.4). • Incorporate other contexts outside of genetics to be used with the statistical outcomes—for example, analyzing baseball players for a new team.

Lessons		
Surface	**Deep**	**Transfer**
• Conduct informational-writing activities (students compare pieces of writing in terms of effectiveness in multiple contexts, with all examples being outside science). • Conduct a review session on adaptations from ecology, and discuss pressures that created change over time (some neutral, some positive, and some negative for species); relate adaptation learning to genetics. • Conduct mathematics lessons on inferential statistics, using examples outside of life and physical science.	• Present statistics problems that include genetics as the context. Have students work through each problem and discuss the statistics and genetics and how they would present their solutions through informational writing.	• Have students review multiple case studies and work with others to determine the probability that a variable will impact a larger population.

How will you launch transfer-level work with students? [Narrative]

This unit begins with a specific context associated with genetic mutations. Provide students with a specific genetic disease, and ask that they identify the most current research on the disease (specifically related to forecasting the chances of getting and passing on the disease), questions that are still being asked about the disease or genetic variation in general, and potential ways of better forecasting the disease in future populations. From there, students begin developing surface- and deep-level knowledge through reading, writing, and talking for all core outcomes.

Source for standard: NGA & CCSSO, 2010a, 2010b.

Teaching-for-Transfer Unit of Learning

Learning Intention

Students will:

- Describe, analyze, and evaluate the impact of monopolies on society and the economy

Success Criteria

Surface

Students will:

- Define *monopoly*
- Define *monopoly power*
- List the sources of monopoly power
- Explain barriers to entry and exit
- Draw and explain monopolist revenue curves
- Identify welfare loss and surplus in a monopoly
- List the means of limiting monopolies
- Define *natural monopoly*
- Identify means of regulating a natural monopoly (that is, marginal cost and average cost pricing)

Deep

Students will:

- Calculate profit and revenue maximization from data
- Evaluate profit and revenue maximization as a means for monopolist decision making
- Describe the strengths and challenges of a monopoly
- Compare and contrast monopoly with perfect competition

Transfer Success Criteria

Students will:

- Present and evaluate a solution that a government could use in the face of a monopoly
- Evaluate the efficiency of different monopolies

Contexts	
	- John D. Rockefeller and Standard Oil
	- Walmart
	- Microsoft
	- Tennessee Valley Authority
	- Moscow Metro
	- Lemonade stand
	- YKK
	- Pacific Gas and Electric Company (PG&E)

Questions		
Surface	**Deep**	**Transfer (Driving Questions)**
- To what extent are monopolies efficient? - To what extent should monopolies be regulated?	- Why do unregulated monopolies cause problems for others? - Why does regulation not serve as a purely ideal solution to the challenges of monopolies	- Who should regulate monopolies? - Where do the characteristics of monopolies occur in other aspects of society?

Tasks		
Surface	**Deep**	**Transfer (Products, Performances, and Portfolios)**

Students will:
 	
• Do a knowledge check
  – Definitions
  – Diagrams
• Write about an example in Padlet that represents the assumptions of monopoly
• Find a business that holds a lot of monopoly power and explain how it holds it
• Describe an appropriate government response to limit that monopoly power
	Students will:
	
	• Explain revenue maximization in relation to a drawn diagram
	• Create a mark scheme for the prompt "Evaluate profit and revenue maximization as a means for monopolist decision making"
	• List the pros and cons of a monopoly
		Students will:
		
		• Argue for and against a monopoly
		• Compare and contrast monopoly with perfect competition (paper 1 style)

Incorporating Perspective and Perplexity	
Perspective	**Perplexity**
• Present students with different perspectives; for example, have them evaluate monopolies from the positions of those within an organization as well as stakeholders directly or indirectly impacted by the organization (customer, CEO, employee, shareholder, government agency, president or prime minister, and politician running for election).	• Present to students a change in the context during the unit. • Present to students an unforeseen event (for example, new technology, a forest fire, or an interest-rate change).

Lessons		
Surface	**Deep**	**Transfer**
• Students are presented with surface-level knowledge through direct instruction lessons (including guided and independent practice).	• Students engage in a gallery walk and jigsaw and consultancy protocols.	• Students review multiple case studies and identify the key problem, propose a solution, and present their case to other students.

How will you launch transfer-level work with students? [Narrative]

Present students with a case study regarding a monopoly. Students must decide whether a fictitious organization's decision to acquire another organization is beneficial for the company, customers, and the greater community. Then ask students to explain their answers and the rationale for their decisions. Provide key success criteria and tasks that allow students to evaluate their previous answers after learning core knowledge related to monopolies. As students go through surface- and deep-level lessons, they face multiple perspective shifts and perplexing variables that require them to focus on breadth and depth in order for them to make an informed analysis and perhaps change their initial decision.

Figure C.8: Eleventh-grade near transfer.

REFERENCES AND RESOURCES

Almarode, J., & Vandas, K. (2018). *Clarity for learning: Five essential practices that empower students and teachers.* Thousand Oaks, CA: Corwin Press.

Argyris, C., & Schön, D. A. (1996). *Organizational learning: Theory, method, and practice* (Vol. 2). Reading, MA: Addison-Wesley.

Arnolda, G., Chien, T. D., Hayen, A., Xuan Hoi, N. T., Maningas, K., Joe, P., et al. (2018). A comparison of the effectiveness of three LED phototherapy machines, single- and double-sided, for treating neonatal jaundice in a low resource setting. *PLoS ONE, 13*(10). Accessed at https://journals.plos.org/plosone/article?id=10.1371/journal.pone.0205432 on May 4, 2020.

Bahcall, S. (2019). *Loonshots: How to nurture the crazy ideas that win wars, cure diseases, and transform industries.* New York: St. Martin's Press.

Biggs, J. B. (2003). *Teaching for quality learning at university: What the student does* (2nd ed.). Philadelphia: Open University Press.

Biggs, J. B., & Collis, K. F. (1982). *Evaluating the quality of learning: The SOLO taxonomy.* New York: Academic Press.

Brookfield, S. (1986). *Understanding and facilitating adult learning: A comprehensive analysis of principles and effective practices.* San Francisco: Jossey-Bass.

California Department of Education. (2000). *History–social science content standards for California public schools, kindergarten through grade twelve.* Sacramento, CA: Author. Accessed at www.cde.ca.gov/be/st/ss/documents/histsocscistnd.pdf on January 7, 2020.

Cepeda, N. J., Vul, E., Rohrer, D., Wixted, J. T., & Pashler, H. (2008). Spacing effects in learning: A temporal ridgeline of optimal retention. *Psychological Science, 19*(11), 1095–1102.

Clarke, S. (2014). *Outstanding formative assessment: Culture and practice.* Philadelphia: Trans-Atlantic.

Claxton, G. (2017). *The learning power approach: Teaching learners to teach themselves.* Thousand Oaks, CA: Corwin Press.

Cooper, A. (2018, April 2). *MPSF speaker series: Anderson Cooper.* Conducted at the Marin Veterans' Memorial Auditorium in San Rafael, CA.

de Bono, E. (1999). *Six thinking hats.* Boston: Back Bay Books.

Drexler, M. (2008, December 15). Looking under the hood and seeing an incubator. *The New York Times.* Accessed at www.nytimes.com/2008/12/16/health/16incubators.html on May 4, 2020.

Dumaine, B. (1994, September 5). The trouble with teams. *Fortune, 130*(5), 86–88, 90, 92.

Duncker, K. (1945). On problem solving. (L. S. Lees, Trans.). *Psychological Monographs, 58*(5), i–113.

Dunne, F., Evans, P., & Thompson-Grove, G. (2017, March 30). *Consultancy protocol: Framing consultancy dilemmas.* Accessed at www.schoolreforminitiative.org /download/consultancy on January 7, 2020.

Dweck, C. S. (2006). *Mindset: The new psychology of success.* New York: Random House.

EL Education. (n.d.). *Jigsaw protocol.* Accessed at https://eleducation.org/uploads /downloads/ELED-JigsawProtocol-012816.pdf on January 13, 2020.

Epstein, D. (2019). *Range: Why generalists triumph in a specialized world.* New York: Riverhead Books.

Fisher, D., Frey, N., & Hattie, J. (2017). *Teaching literacy in the visible learning classroom, grades K–5.* Thousand Oaks, CA: Corwin Press.

Gardner, H. (1999). *The disciplined mind: What all students should understand.* New York: Simon & Schuster.

Geary, D. C., & Berch, D. B. (Eds.). (2016). *Evolutionary perspectives on child development and education.* New York: Springer.

Gentner, D., Holyoak, K. J., & Kokinov, B. N. (Eds.). (2001). *The analogical mind: Perspectives from cognitive science.* Cambridge, MA: MIT Press.

George, M. L., Rowlands, D., Price, M., & Maxey, J. (2004). *The lean Six Sigma pocket toolbook: A quick reference guide to nearly 100 tools for improving process quality, speed, and complexity.* New York: McGraw-Hill.

Gick, M. L., & Holyoak, K. J. (1980). Analogical problem solving. *Cognitive Psychology, 12*(3), 306–355.

Gick, M. L., & Holyoak, K. J. (1983). Schema induction and analogical transfer. *Cognitive Psychology, 15*(1), 1–38.

Gladwell, M. (2013, June 17). The gift of doubt: Albert O. Hirschman and the power of failure. *The New Yorker.* Accessed at www.newyorker.com/magazine/2013/06/24/the -gift-of-doubt on November 13, 2019.

Gross, T. (2019, January 30). *"Beale Street" and "Vice" composer isn't afraid to play the "wrong" notes.* Accessed at www.npr.org/2019/01/30/689822798/beale-street-and -vice-composer-isn-t-afraid-to-play-the-wrong-notes on December 12, 2019.

Guskey, T. R. (Ed.). (2009). *The teacher as assessment leader.* Bloomington, IN: Solution Tree Press.

Harford, T. (2015, September). *How frustration can make us more creative* [Video file]. Accessed at www.ted.com/talks/tim_harford_how_frustration_can_make_us_more _creative?language=en on December 19, 2019.

Harvey, T. R., Bearley, W. L., & Corkrum, S. M. (2002). *The practical decision maker: A handbook for decision making and problem solving in organizations.* Lanham, MD: Scarecrow Press.

Hasso Plattner Institute of Design at Stanford University. (2020). *Get started with design thinking.* Accessed at https://dschool.stanford.edu/resources/getting-started-with -design-thinking on March 2, 2020.

Hattie, J. (2009). *Visible learning: A synthesis of over 800 meta-analyses relating to achievement.* New York: Routledge.

Hattie, J. (2012). *Visible learning for teachers: Maximizing impact on learning.* New York: Routledge.

Hattie, J. (2015). The applicability of visible learning to higher education. *Scholarship of Teaching and Learning in Psychology, 1*(1), 79–91.

Hattie, J., & Clarke, S. (2018). *Visible learning: Feedback.* New York: Routledge.

Hattie, J., & Donoghue, G. M. (2016). Learning strategies: A synthesis and conceptual model. *Science of Learning, 1.* https://doi.org/10.1038/npjscilearn.2016.13

Heflebower, T. (2005). *An educator's perception of STARS from Nebraska education service unit staff developers* (Unpublished doctoral dissertation). University of Nebraska– Lincoln. Accessed at http://digitalcommons.unl.edu/dissertations/AAI3194116 on June 8, 2020.

Heflebower, T., Hoegh, J. K., & Warrick, P. B. (2014). *A school leader's guide to standards- based grading.* Bloomington, IN: Marzano Resources.

Heflebower, T., Hoegh, J. K., Warrick, P. B., & Flygare, J. (2019). *A teacher's guide to standards-based learning.* Bloomington, IN: Marzano Resources.

Johnson, S. (2010). *Where good ideas come from: The natural history of innovation.* New York: Riverhead Books.

Johnson, S. (2014). *How we got to now: Six innovations that made the modern world.* New York: Riverhead Books.

Keynes, J. M. (1930). *Economic possibilities for our grandchildren.* Accessed at www.econ .yale.edu/smith/econ116a/keynes1.pdf on November 13, 2019.

Keynes, J. M. (2018). *The general theory of employment, interest and money.* London: Palgrave Macmillan. (Original work published 1936)

Koestler, A. (1964). *The act of creation.* New York: Macmillan.

Lee, H. (1960). *To kill a mockingbird.* Philadelphia: J. B. Lippincott.

Liker, J. K. (2004). *The Toyota way: 14 management principles from the world's greatest manufacturer.* New York: McGraw-Hill.

Margolis, J. D., & Stoltz, P. G. (2010). How to bounce back from adversity. *Harvard Business Review, 88*(1–2), 86–92.

Marzano, R. J. (1992). *A different kind of classroom: Teaching with dimensions of learning.* Alexandria, VA: Association for Supervision and Curriculum Development.

Marzano, R. J. (2009). *Designing and teaching learning goals and objectives.* Bloomington, IN: Marzano Resources.

Marzano, R. J. (2010). *Formative assessment and standards-based grading.* Bloomington, IN: Marzano Resources.

Marzano, R. J. (2017). *The new art and science of teaching.* Bloomington, IN: Solution Tree Press.

Marzano, R. J., & Heflebower, T. (2012). *Teaching and assessing 21st century skills*. Bloomington, IN: Marzano Resources.

Marzano, R. J., Pickering, D. J., & Pollock, J. E. (2001). *Classroom instruction that works: Research-based strategies for increasing student achievement*. Alexandria, VA: Association for Supervision and Curriculum Development.

Marzano, R. J., & Simms, J. A. (2013). *Coaching classroom instruction*. Bloomington, IN: Marzano Resources.

Marzano, R. J., Warrick, P. B., Rains, C. L., & DuFour, R. (2018). *Leading a high reliability school*. Bloomington, IN: Solution Tree Press.

Marzano, R. J., & Waters, T. (2009). *District leadership that works: Striking the right balance*. Bloomington, IN: Solution Tree Press.

McDonald, J., & Allen, D. (2017, March 30). *Tuning protocol*. Accessed at www.schoolreforminitiative.org/download/tuning-protocol on January 8, 2020.

McDowell, M. (2017). *Rigorous PBL by design: Three design shifts for developing confident and competent learners*. Thousand Oaks, CA: Corwin Press.

McDowell, M. (2018). *The lead learner: Improving clarity, coherence, and capacity for all*. Thousand Oaks, CA: Corwin Press.

McDowell, M. (2019). *Developing expert learners: A roadmap for growing confident and competent students*. Thousand Oaks, CA: Corwin Press.

McGrath, C. (2012, December 19). Quentin's world. *The New York Times*. Accessed at http://mobile.nytimes.com/2012/12/23/movies/how-quentin-tarantino-concocted-a-genre-of-his-own.html on November 13, 2019.

McTighe, J. (2018). Three key questions on measuring learning. *Educational Leadership*, *75*(5), 14–20.

McTighe, J., & Wiggins, G. (2013). *Essential questions: Opening doors to student understanding*. Alexandria, VA: Association for Supervision and Curriculum Development.

Michaels, S., & O'Connor, C. (2012). *Talk science primer*. Cambridge, MA: TERC. Accessed at https://inquiryproject.terc.edu/shared/pd/TalkScience_Primer.pdf on November 13, 2019.

Minervino, R. A., Olguín, V., & Trench, M. (2017). Promoting interdomain analogical transfer: When creating a problem helps to solve a problem. *Memory & Cognition*, *45*(2), 221–232.

Miranda, L. M. (2015). The room where it happens [Recorded by L. Odom Jr., L. M. Miranda, D. Diggs, & O. Onaodowan]. On *Hamilton* [CD]. New York: Atlantic.

Muller, D. A. (2008). *Designing effective multimedia for physics education* (Doctoral dissertation). University of Sydney, Australia. Accessed at https://sydney.edu.au/science/physics/pdfs/research/super/PhD(Muller).pdf on November 13, 2019.

National Governors Association Center for Best Practices & Council of Chief State School Officers. (2010a). *Common Core State Standards for English language arts and literacy in history/social studies, science, and technical subjects*. Washington, DC: Authors. Accessed at www.corestandards.org/assets/CCSSI_ELA%20Standards.pdf on January 7, 2020.

National Governors Association Center for Best Practices & Council of Chief State School Officers. (2010b). *Common Core State Standards for mathematics*. Washington, DC: Authors. Accessed at www.corestandards.org/assets/CCSSI_Math%20 Standards.pdf on January 7, 2020.

NGSS Lead States. (2013). *Next Generation Science Standards: For states, by states*. Washington, DC: The National Academies Press.

Nottingham, J. (2017). *The learning challenge: How to guide your students through the learning pit to achieve deeper understanding*. Thousand Oaks, CA: Corwin Press.

Nuthall, G. (2007). *The hidden lives of learners*. Wellington, New Zealand: NZCER Press.

Nutt, P. C. (2002). *Why decisions fail: Avoiding the blunders and traps that lead to debacles*. San Francisco: Berrett-Koehler.

Orange, T. (2018). *There there*. New York: Knopf.

Perkins, D. N., & Salomon, G. (1994). Transfer of learning. In T. Husén & T. N. Postlethwaite (Eds.), *International encyclopedia of education* (2nd ed., pp. 6452–6456). Oxford, England: Pergamon.

Prestero, T. (2012, June). *Design for people, not awards* [Video file]. Accessed at www.ted .com/talks/timothy_prestero_design_for_people_not_awards?language=en on May 4, 2020.

Recht, D. R., & Leslie, L. (1988). Effect of prior knowledge on good and poor readers' memory of text. *Journal of Educational Psychology, 80*(1), 16–20.

Reeves, D. B. (2013). *Leading change in your school: How to conquer myths, build commitment, and get results*. Alexandria, VA: Association for Supervision and Curriculum Development.

Roberton, F. (2013). *A tale of two beasts*. La Jolla, CA: Kane Miller.

Robson, D. (2019). *The intelligence trap: Why smart people make dumb mistakes*. New York: W. W. Norton.

Rothermel, R. C. (1993, May). *Mann Gulch fire: A race that couldn't be won* (General Technical Report INT-299). Ogden, UT: U.S. Department of Agriculture, Forest Service, Intermountain Research Station.

Sala, G., & Gobet, F. (2017). Does far transfer exist? Negative evidence from chess, music, and working memory training. *Current Directions in Psychological Science, 26*(6), 515–520.

Schwarz, R. (2013). *Smart leaders, smarter teams: How you and your team get unstuck to get results*. San Francisco: Jossey-Bass.

Schwarz, R. (2017). *The skilled facilitator: A comprehensive resource for consultants, facilitators, coaches, and trainers* (3rd ed.). Hoboken, NJ: Jossey-Bass.

Simstrom, L. (2019, February 22). *What an insect can teach us about adapting to stress*. Accessed at www.npr.org/sections/health-shots/2019/02/22/696894502/what-an -insect-can-teach-us-about-adapting-to-stress on November 13, 2019.

Sweller, J., van Merriënboer, J. J. G., & Paas, F. (2019). Cognitive architecture and instructional design: 20 years later. *Educational Psychology Review, 31*(2), 261–292. https://doi.org/10.1007/s10648-019-09465-5

Thomas, E. J., Brunsting, J. R., & Warrick, P. L. (2010). *Styles and strategies for teaching high school mathematics: 21 techniques for differentiating instruction and assessment.* Thousand Oaks, CA: Corwin Press.

Tolentino, J. (2018, May 7). The promise of vaping and the rise of Juul. *The New Yorker.* Accessed at www.newyorker.com/magazine/2018/05/14/the-promise-of-vaping-and -the-rise-of-juul on November 13, 2019.

Wexler, N. (2019). *The knowledge gap: The hidden cause of America's broken education system—and how to fix it.* New York: Avery.

Wiggins, G., & McTighe, J. (2007). *Schooling by design: Mission, action, and achievement.* Alexandria, VA: Association for Supervision and Curriculum Development.

Wiliam, D. (2018a). *Creating the schools our children need: Why what we're doing now won't help much (and what we can do instead).* West Palm Beach, FL: Learning Sciences International.

Wiliam, D. (2018b). *Embedded formative assessment* (2nd ed.). Bloomington, IN: Solution Tree Press.

Willingham, D. (2009). *Why don't students like school? A cognitive scientist answers questions about how the mind works and what it means for the classroom.* San Francisco: Jossey-Bass.

Willingham, D. (2018, February 11). *A new idea to promote transfer* [Blog post]. Accessed at www.danielwillingham.com/daniel-willingham-science-and-education-blog/a-new -idea-to-promote-transfer on November 13, 2019.

World Café Community Foundation. (2015). *A quick reference guide for hosting World Café.* Accessed at www.theworldcafe.com/wp-content/uploads/2015/07/Cafe-To-Go -Revised.pdf on March 3, 2020.

Youssef-Shalala, A., Ayres, P., Schubert, C., & Sweller, J. (2014). Using a general problem-solving strategy to promote transfer. *Journal of Experimental Psychology: Applied, 20*(3), 215–231.

Zhao, Y. (2012). *World class learners: Educating creative and entrepreneurial students.* Thousand Oaks, CA: Corwin Press.

INDEX

Praise for

Teaching for Transfer

"Surely the aim of schooling is to teach students skills, knowledge, and understanding *so that* they can transfer these to new situations. So often, students are told, 'You need to learn this so you can use it in real life or in your future career,' and so often, teachers seek 'authentic' contexts, aiming to minimize the distance between learning the skills and applying them to transfer situations. It is probably our dirtiest secret in education that we all know this to be a truism, but rarely do we see evidence as to how best to teach transfer. Sadly, we work backward and claim students who can transfer are bright or have high levels of self-regulation, inferring that these skills to transfer is a function of the person, and we use more pejorative words for those who do not have these skills. Instead, the question should be how to teach all students the skills of transfer—they are teachable skills, right?

"McDowell takes on the toughest question in our business—how to teach for transfer. For boldness alone, this book is worth savoring, but it also includes many techniques and tools for teachers to consider as they are asked to deliberately teach the skills of transfer. He makes it very clear that transfer is built on knowledge and understanding and that teaching for transfer can be built into the everyday life of the classroom.

"McDowell uses Biggs and Collis's (1982) SOLO model to highlight that transfer is built on surface and deep knowledge, and he reminds us of the important distinction between near, near-to-far, and far transfer. The major point is made that while 'surface-and-deep networks are often associated with understanding and recycling old ideas, transfer networks are related to reconfiguring and rearranging surface and deep knowledge within and across disciplines to find creative ways to solve problems.' We can often see illustrations of near transfer, but so much less do we see near-to-far or far transfer. Indeed, the current grammar of schooling is embedded with surface knowledge in the conspiracy that students . . . prefer this grammar—lots of teaching talk, a focus on the facts, and assignments that are more closed than open. This is despite our rhetoric as teachers, curriculum developers, measurement makers, and politicians, proclaiming that schools are preparing for life and teaching transferable skills and that we all should care deeply and passionately about what is taught in our schools. The rhetoric is miles from the reality. But attending more to near and far transfer would add a richness that might entice more students to welcome coming to school and invest in school learning.

"Another of John Biggs's (2003) contributions is the model of constructive alignment. There is a need to align the rhetoric, the content, the assignment, the assessment, the scoring, and the feedback—and this McDowell accomplishes in chapter 1, with anchor and best-fit strategies. It entails being clear about the focus on transfer in the learning intentions and success criteria; explicitly providing multiple contexts to engage in surface, deep, and transfer learning intentions and success criteria by constructing questions at the transfer level of learning; and co-developing transfer-level challenges and tasks.

"Throughout this book, it is never presumed that teaching for transfer is easy, particularly when the skills required are demanding; there is a need for sufficient levels of surface and deep knowing and understanding; there is the element of the unknown, as the bridge from the known to the new (the far) is sometimes scary and requires developing high levels of confidence in taking on such challenges; it requires looking at known knowledge from new perspectives; it demands high skills in detecting similarities and differences in problem specifications; and often, transfer requires high levels of problem solving and creativity. High demands indeed. It reminds me of my favorite definition of *creativity* by Arthur Koestler (1964) as the bringing together of two or more seemingly unrelated ideas, but in the case of transfer, it goes a step further and asks that the ideas build a bridge from the productive application of prior learning and experiences to novel contexts. McDowell explores this leap using the core processes relating to activation, application, and authenticity.

"There are so many questions that come from these chapters on transfer. Is teaching for transfer as simple as changing the context and asking students to try to apply their knowledge and skills to this new context (very common in math problems), or do we just wait to see what is retained and see if students can recall prior knowing in new tasks? Should teachers directly guide and engage their students in the desired target performance and thus promote reflexive transfer (what Perkins and Salomon [1994] call *hugging*) or intentionally encourage abstractions of general rules so that they are less context dependent (*bridging*)? Maybe transfer can negatively influence subsequent performance by not developing new knowledge and understanding to add to prior generalizations, and we all know the times when we bring our prior understanding to a new situation and it is the wrong application of this prior knowledge and can lead to misconceptions, overgeneralization, and errors. So many breakthroughs in new knowledge occur when we pause to ask, 'Do our prior understandings and generalizations need to be questioned in this new context?' McDowell notes how important it is to prompt students to explain why and how they have come to generalized principles and what evidence they can provide to support these principles as a core part of the skills of transfer.

"Transfer is a process, not an end point, as once we have transferred our knowledge and understanding to a new situation, we are then ready to commence the cycle again from surface to deep to transfer. But the beauty of the arguments throughout this book is that they value the learning of skills, the skills of understanding, and the understanding of applying our learning to near- and far-transfer problems. These three parts of the instructional cycle need to be ever present in success criteria, in the tasks, and in the assessment as typical parts of the class experience. My hope is for more discussion about transfer, greater levels of research, more resources for and evaluations of the teaching of transfer in our classes, and deeper investigation of the thinking process of students when engaged in transfer—this book will be a major catalyst for these new ventures."

—John Hattie
Laureate Professor, Melbourne Graduate School of Education

"We have learned the importance of surface, deep, and transfer learning, and that *rigor* is 'the equal intensity and integration' of all three. Still, leaders continue to ask, 'How and when do we teach to transfer?' Thus, McDowell's book is timely and needed! In the book, he writes, 'Transfer is fundamentally built on change.' He offers many visuals, examples, and reflective questions that will guide teams to ensure these opportunities are prioritized for our learners. Most importantly, as a former history teacher at heart, I believe this book is absolutely essential given the current situation in our world amid a pandemic and protests that call for radical change to end racism. Teachers must provide an environment that intentionally promotes teaching for transfer if we are going to ensure positive and lasting change for our future generations."

—LeeAnn Aguilar-Lawlor
Superintendent, Cartwright School District, Phoenix, Arizona

"*Teaching for Transfer* is a book I have been waiting for, as it outlines so clearly how students can experience learning on deeper and deeper levels. The book gets to that age-old dilemma 'How deep should instruction go?' Do we teach the building blocks, skills, and concepts of what is expected, or do we stretch students' thinking by grappling with real-world problems—or both? If you wish to better understand and harness the process of learning, this book is for you!"

—Kara Vandas
Author and Educational Consultant

"The terms *surface learning* and *deep learning* are increasingly well used in education yet are but two of the learning triumvirate; the third is *transfer*. Indeed, it could be said that it is only when transfer occurs that learning sticks. With transfer, learning is applied appropriately to new contexts and therefore becomes much more enduring. This is what makes Michael McDowell's *Teaching for Transfer* so important and timely. He shows, in his own inimitable style, exactly how to teach your students skills of transfer so that their learning might be more robust and sustainable."

—James Nottingham
Founder, Challenging Learning; Creator, the Learning Pit

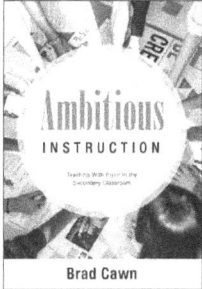

Ambitious Instruction
Brad Cawn

Ensure all learners have opportunities to engage deeply in meaningful intellectual work. In *Ambitious Instruction*, author Brad Cawn offers a blueprint for how to make rigor visible, accessible, and actionable in grade 6–12 classrooms. The resource guides readers toward using the twin tenets of problem-based learning and synthesis to significantly strengthen students' ability to read, write, and think within and across disciplines.
BKF842

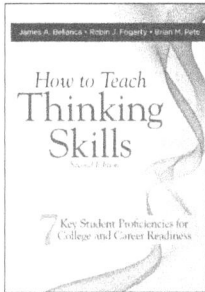

How to Teach Thinking Skills, Second Edition
James A. Bellanca, Robin J. Fogarty, and Brian M. Pete

Ensure your students develop the higher-order, complex thinking skills they need to not just survive but thrive in a 21st century world. The latest edition of this best-selling guide details a practical, three-phase teaching model and dives deep into seven essential student proficiencies.
BKF900

Growing Tomorrow's Citizens in Today's Classrooms
Cassandra Erkens, Tom Schimmer, and Nicole Dimich Vagle

For students to succeed in today's ever-changing world, they must acquire unique knowledge and skills. Practical and research-based, this resource will help educators design assessment and instruction to ensure students master critical competencies, including collaboration, critical thinking, creative thinking, communication, digital citizenship, and more.
BKF765

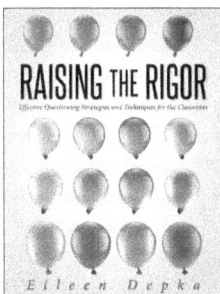

Raising the Rigor: Effective Questioning Strategies and Techniques for the Classroom
Eileen Depka

This user-friendly resource shares questioning strategies and techniques proven to enhance students' critical thinking skills, deepen their engagement, and better prepare them for college and careers. The author also provides a range of templates, surveys, and checklists for planning instruction, deconstructing academic standards, and increasing classroom rigor.
BKF722

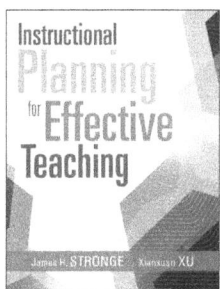

Instructional Planning for Effective Teaching
James H. Stronge and Xianxuan Xu

Explore research-based instructional planning tools teachers, leaders, and administrators can use in everyday practice. Discover powerful strategies and guidelines for developing quality lessons, setting learning objectives, planning differentiated instruction, and designing technology-integrated learning to effectively teach and challenge every student.
BKF642

Solution Tree | Press

a division of
Solution Tree

Wait! Your professional development journey doesn't have to end with the last pages of this book.

We realize improving student learning doesn't happen overnight. And your school or district shouldn't be left to puzzle out all the details of this process alone.

No matter where you are on the journey, we're committed to helping you get to the next stage.

Take advantage of everything from **custom workshops** to **keynote presentations** and **interactive web and video conferencing**. We can even help you develop an action plan tailored to fit your specific needs.

Let's get the conversation started.

Call 888.763.9045 today.

SolutionTree.com

www.ingramcontent.com/pod-product-compliance
Lightning Source LLC
Chambersburg PA
CBHW081435270326
41932CB00019B/3210